Treble Recorder Technique

by
Alan Davis

NOVELLO

Printed in Great Britain

Cat. No. 12 0545 05

ISBN 0 85360 117 8

Contents

Introduction

The recorder is an instrument of great antiquity. Numerous medieval paintings and carvings testify to the existence of instruments of the recorder type – an end-blown whistle with seven finger holes and a thumb-hole; unfortunately none of these early recorders seems to have survived. Specimens have survived from the Renaissance in significant numbers, however, and may be seen in many museums throughout Europe. Renaissance recorders were usually made in one piece with a more or less cylindrical bore, giving a compass of about an octave and a half and having a full, rather solemn tone which is ideally suited to the consort music of the sixteenth century. Modern recorders built on the Renaissance pattern can be obtained quite easily, though few of those available could be described as exact copies of original instruments.

In the second half of the seventeenth century a group of French instrument makers brought about revolutionary changes in the design of all the woodwind instruments. The recorder was then made in two or three sections with a bore which tapered towards the foot of the instrument. It had a fully chromatic compass of two octaves with a few additional higher notes, and a bright, reedy tone well suited to solo playing. Recorders were still made in various sizes but the alto instrument in F, known in England as the treble, was the one most frequently used. It was known by a variety of names including 'flauto' (the most common), 'flauto dolce', 'English flute', 'common flute', 'Blockflöte' and 'flûte à bec'. Until about 1750 the flute was always referred to specifically as 'flauto traverso', 'flûte traversière', 'German flute' or 'Querflöte'.

After a period of equality with the flute, during which time a huge quantity of music was written for it, the recorder declined steadily in popularity. Composers in the *galant* style preferred the more expressive, romantic tone of the flute, and by the end of the eighteenth century the recorder had become virtually obsolete. There was a certain amount of interest in the recorder in academic circles in the late nineteenth century but it was not until the 1920s that Arnold Dolmetsch began to make the first modern recorders. Most recorders today are based on the baroque instrument but are intended for use in a wide range of musical styles and therefore differ from the originals in details of pitch, tuning, voicing and fingering. More faithful copies of old instruments can also be obtained from a few specialist makers.

Since the early days of the recorder revival the instrument has been used increasingly in performances of appropriate music from the baroque period and earlier besides attracting living composers to write for it in a variety of idioms, the most advanced of which have extended its range and technique. The recorder has an unrivalled reputation as the ideal instrument for educational and amateur music making while still presenting a worthy challenge to the aspiring virtuoso.

This book is intended primarily for recorder players who wish to attain sufficient technical ability to explore the large repertoire of solo and chamber music for the treble recorder, and secondly for those who teach the recorder in schools and elsewhere and who, though they may not aspire to a high standard of performance themselves, are nevertheless anxious to acquire an introduction to good technique and an understanding of the recorder's potential as a serious musical instrument. Much of the recorder music published is intended for use in schools, and instruction books are often written in terms of the descant recorder, an instrument whose authentic solo repertoire is very small. They usually include material selected for its suitability for children and incorporate an introduction to the rudiments of music. In the present work I have attempted to fulfil a need which my own teaching has made apparent by providing a concise but comprehensive tutor of the kind used by students of modern orchestral wind instruments.

Part I is concerned with the basic technique of the modern recorder and consists of graded exercises beginning at an elementary level, scales and arpeggios and advanced technical studies. Part II attempts to relate some of the stylistic problems of the recorder's varied repertoire to the more specialized techniques of the renaissance and baroque recorder and also includes an introduction to *avant-garde* technique.

Acknowledgements

I am indebted to Paul Clark, Colin Hand and David Lindley for their interest and encouragement; to Gordon Saunders for his detailed comments and numerous helpful suggestions; to John Craven for advice on continuo playing; and to my students at the Birmingham School of Music who have contributed so much to the formulation of the ideas in this book.

Alan Davis
25 September 1980

PART I

1 Chart of normal fingerings for the modern recorder

The fingers used in recorder playing are identified as follows:

Left hand

Thumb	–	0
Index finger	–	1
Middle finger	–	2
Ring finger	–	3

Right hand

Index finger	–	4
Middle finger	–	5
Ring finger	–	6
Little finger	–	7

The holes covered to produce any given note can be expressed by a series of figures. A partially covered hole is expressed thus Ø, and a trilling finger thus * (see Section 8).

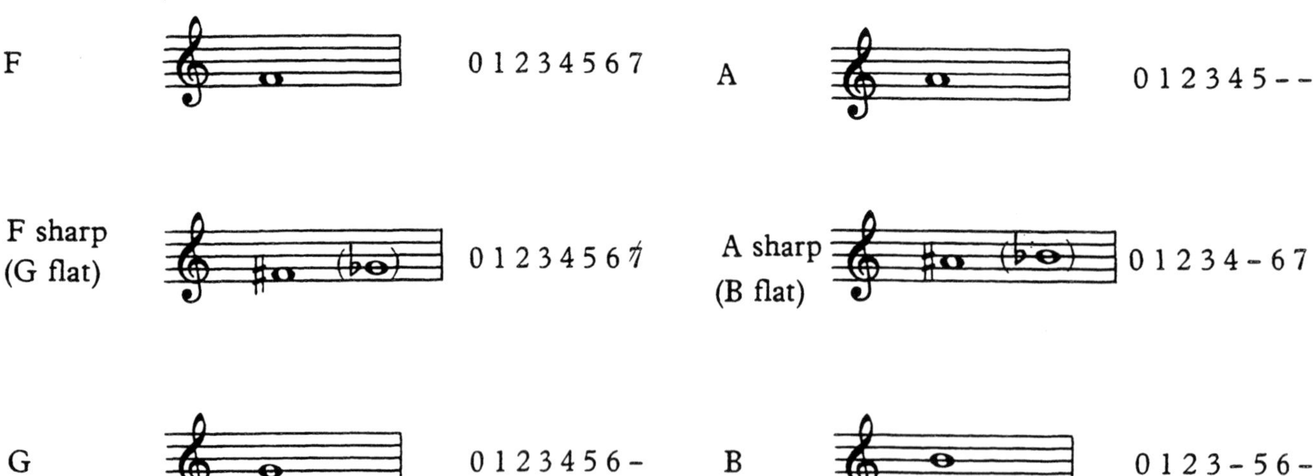

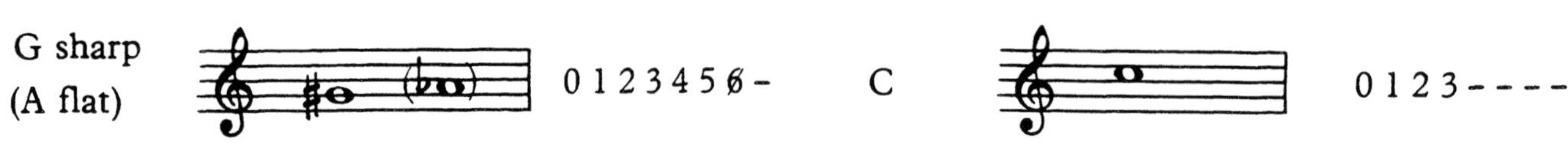

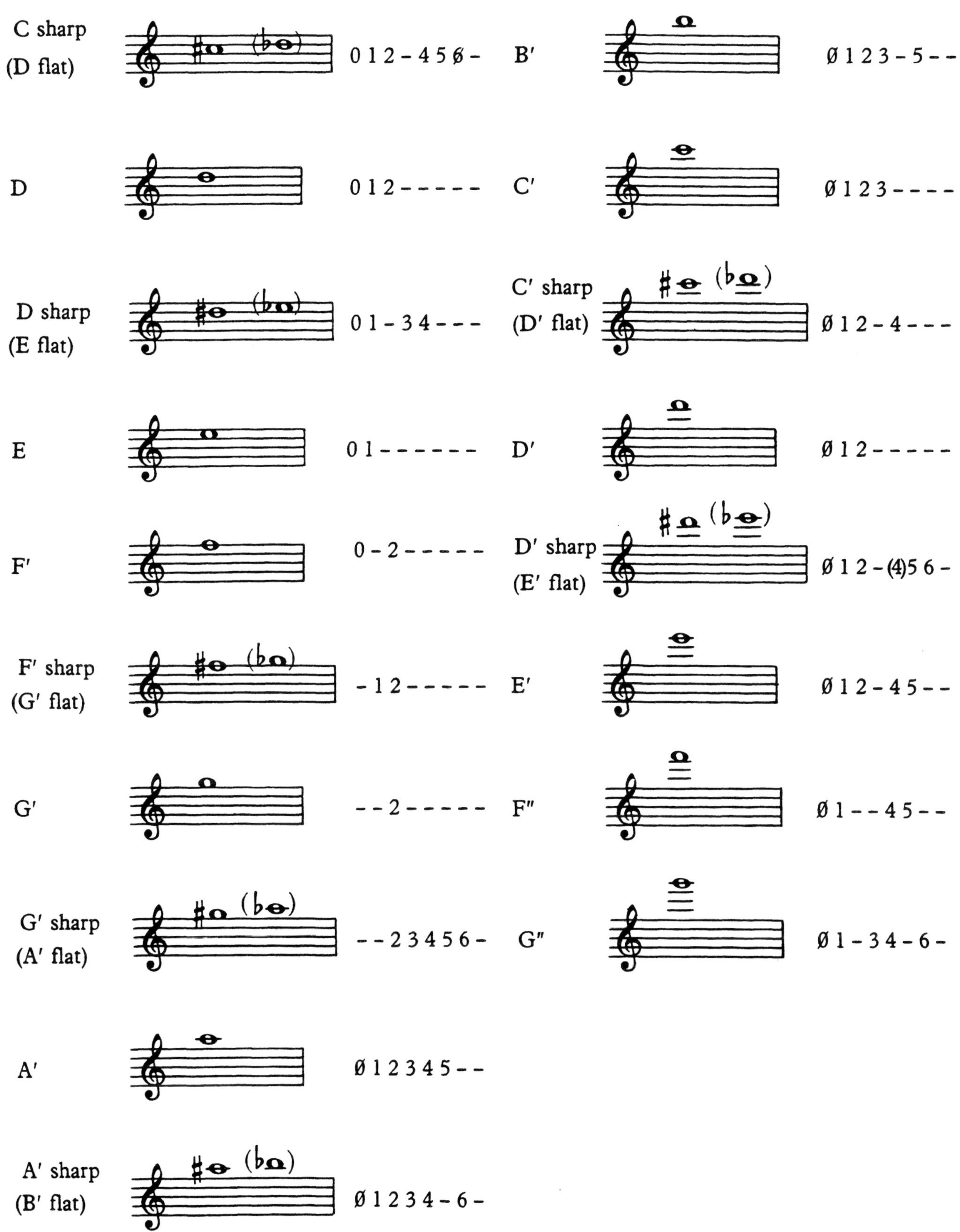
C sharp
(D flat)
0 1 2 – 4 5 6̸ –
D
0 1 2 – – – – –
D sharp
(E flat)
0 1 – 3 4 – – –
E
0 1 – – – – – –
F′
0 – 2 – – – – –
F′ sharp
(G′ flat)
– 1 2 – – – – –
G′
– – 2 – – – – –
G′ sharp
(A′ flat)
– – 2 3 4 5 6 –
A′
Ø 1 2 3 4 5 – –
A′ sharp
(B′ flat)
Ø 1 2 3 4 – 6 –
B′
Ø 1 2 3 – 5 – –
C′
Ø 1 2 3 – – – –
C′ sharp
(D′ flat)
Ø 1 2 – 4 – – –
D′
Ø 1 2 – – – – –
D′ sharp
(E′ flat)
Ø 1 2 – (4) 5 6 –
E′
Ø 1 2 – 4 5 – –
F″
Ø 1 – – 4 5 – –
G″
Ø 1 – 3 4 – 6 –

2 The range and character of the four registers

As can be seen from the fingering chart, the treble recorder has a fully chromatic compass of two octaves from F above middle C together with the high G″. This is the generally accepted 'normal' compass of the instrument, though F″ sharp is possible with difficulty and some higher notes can be produced quite easily. Unlike the modern orchestral woodwind, whose mechanization in the nineteenth century tended to produce a homogeneous tone quality throughout their compass, the recorder's compass divides naturally into four distinct registers, each with its own tonal character. The higher the register the higher the breath pressure necessary for good tone and intonation, but *all* the notes within one register require uniform, or nearly uniform, pressure.

The first register

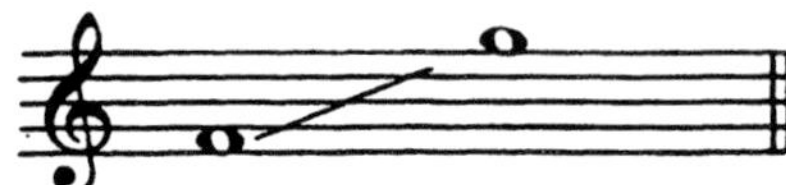

It is commonly supposed that the lowest notes, from F to A or B flat, require gentle breath pressure. In fact, if all the notes of the first register are played with firm, equal breath the low notes will be richer in harmonics and consequently their tone will be more lively and vibrant.

The second register

The second register requires stronger breath pressure than the first for the notes to sound strong and clear as they should. These notes are responsive to variety in articulation and have a certain dynamic flexibility.

The third register

The third register consists of just three notes, all requiring strong breath pressure and accurate positioning of the left thumb. They have a tone which is strong but not always as clear as the second register.

The fourth register

Although G″ is the 'official' top note on the recorder, additional notes in the third octave are possible. The fingerings for these are given in Section 5. The fourth register needs very strong breath pressure and often hard tonguing, producing notes which are loud or even shrill. Their musical usefulness is limited, but in the appropriate context the extreme high notes can sound very effective.

3 The first register

(a) Sustaining and articulating a single note

Apart from the design of the instrument itself, the factor which alone determines the quality of tone produced from the recorder is the way the breath is directed through the windway on to the sharp edge. On other woodwind instruments the airstream is modified by the player's lips forming the so-called *embouchure* but on the recorder this is not possible, while the use of vibrato merely adds another dimension to the tone without altering its essential quality. It follows then that the study of recorder playing should begin with breathing and tone production.

Begin with the note E, fingered with the thumb and index finger of the left hand (0 1 - - - - - -). To sound this note first cover the two holes, steady the instrument with the right thumb, taking care not to cover any extra holes with the unused fingers, and place the mouthpiece gently between the lips. Breathe in and pause, aiming at total bodily relaxation. Place the tip of the tongue on the ridge in the mouth behind the upper front teeth and then remove it from this position gently but quickly, beginning at exactly the same time to breathe out firmly. This should produce the note E. From the outset the following important points should be remembered:

i) The breath should be let out steadily so that the note produced is quite even in tone, with no trace of 'wobble'. This will almost certainly require some practice, indeed, the importance of practising long sustained notes, even for advanced players, can hardly be over-emphasized. It may also be helpful to practise breathing exercises away from the instrument. Relax the body, breathe in slowly and deeply and in so doing expand the rib cage and push the stomach muscles out. This encourages the flattening of the diaphragm so that the lungs are completely filled and the breath is firmly supported. Pause before breathing out, then empty the lungs slowly, allowing a fine, steady stream of air to pass between the lips.

ii) The fingers must cover the holes completely so that no air can escape. Ensure that the fleshy pads and not the tips of the fingers are used.

iii) Avoid a sudden increase or decrease in pressure just before stopping. Simply cut off the air supply by returning the tongue firmly to its original position on the ridge behind the upper teeth.

iv) The tongue movements must be firm and quick but gentle. It is helpful to imagine pronouncing the consonant 'D' to begin a note, but if the action of the tongue is too hard it will produce an unpleasantly harsh effect. (The subject of articulation is dealt with more fully in Section 6.)

EXERCISES

Practise playing long sustained notes and then a series of repeated notes separated by the action of the tongue. The degree of separation can, of course, be varied but in the early stages it should be minimal, the tongue merely touching the ridge momentarily between notes.

1 

Exercises 2 – 5 use repeated notes in various rhythms. Breathe at the places marked ✓; (✓) indicates an optional breath; ✓✓ a big breath. Stop the note before the breath slightly short of its written value, take a quick breath through the sides of the mouth (not through the instrument) and tongue the following note so that it begins correctly in time. The exercises use the note E but may be practised on any note in the first register. In these and subsequent exercises where no indication of speed is given, practise slowly so that any faults may easily be detected and corrected. Gradually increase the speed in any exercise where it seems musically appropriate to do so.

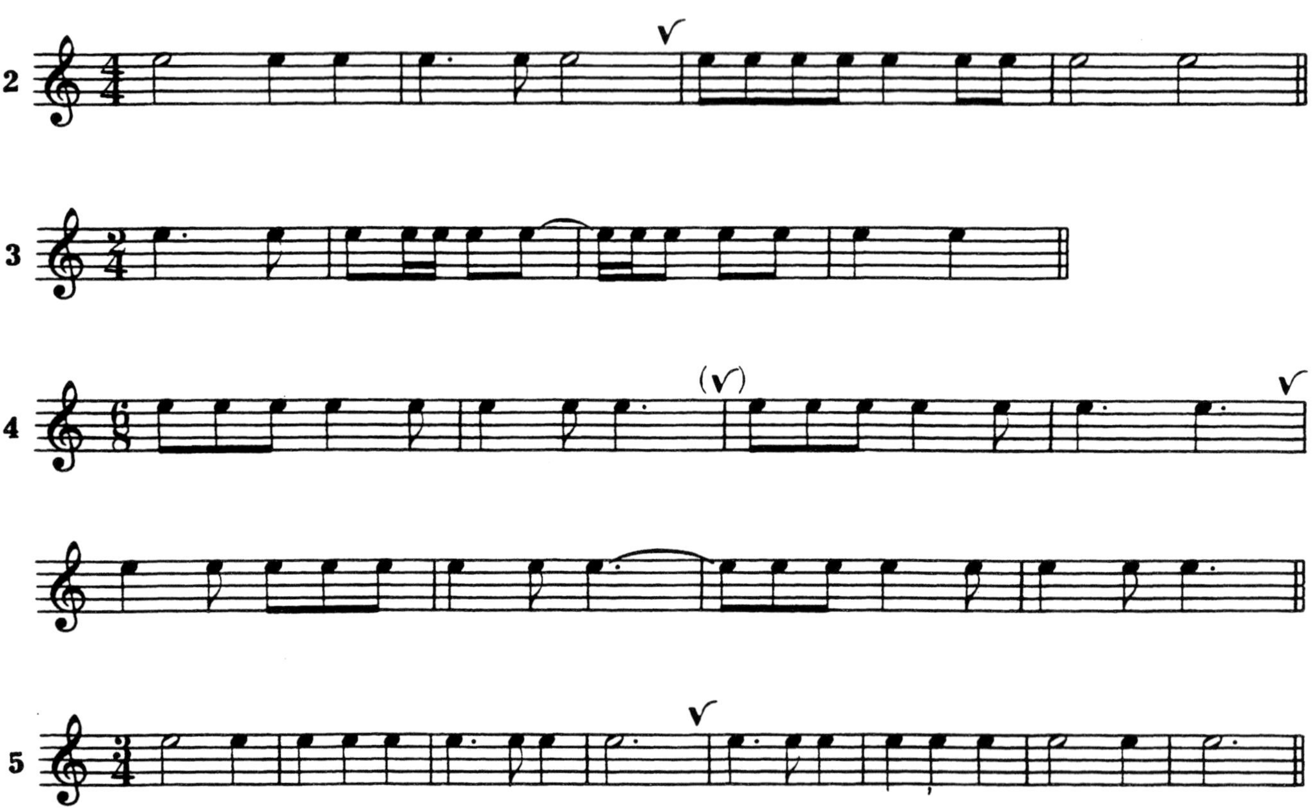

(b) Fingering with the left hand

The finger movements necessary to play a succession of notes of different pitches must combine firmness with economy of movement. Temporarily unused fingers should not be allowed to stray too far from the instrument but should be held poised above their holes at a distance of no more than about half an inch. In the early stages the action of the fingers should be very positive: the covering fingers can gently squeeze the instrument at each change of pitch, but they should remain relaxed and not stiff.

EXERCISES

The curved line in the following exercises is a slur: the tongue is used only to begin the first and stop the last notes enclosed. It follows that the fingers must move with great precision for the exercises to sound smooth and rhythmic. Breathe at the rests, taking care that the preceding note is stopped with the tongue on the beat occupied by the rest.

12

Cross fingering

It is necessary at this stage to consider the principle of cross fingering. Of the notes used in Exercises 1–12 G′ and F′ use *forked fingerings*, that is to say one or more holes are left open above the lowest covered hole. Notes so fingered are usually weaker in tone quality and require softer tonguing than those produced with plain fingerings, though this does not apply to the G′ and F′ just mentioned. When to change from one note to another involves the simultaneous raising and lowering of fingers, as in changing from E to F′, the process is called *cross fingering*. Perfect synchronization of the fingers is necessary and can be achieved only with slow, careful practice. Passages involving cross fingering can sometimes be made easier by the use of alternative fingerings (see Section 8) but no attempt should be made to use these alternatives until the standard fingerings have been learned and mastered.

EXERCISES

13

In Exercises 14–16 cross fingerings are indicated by square brackets.

14
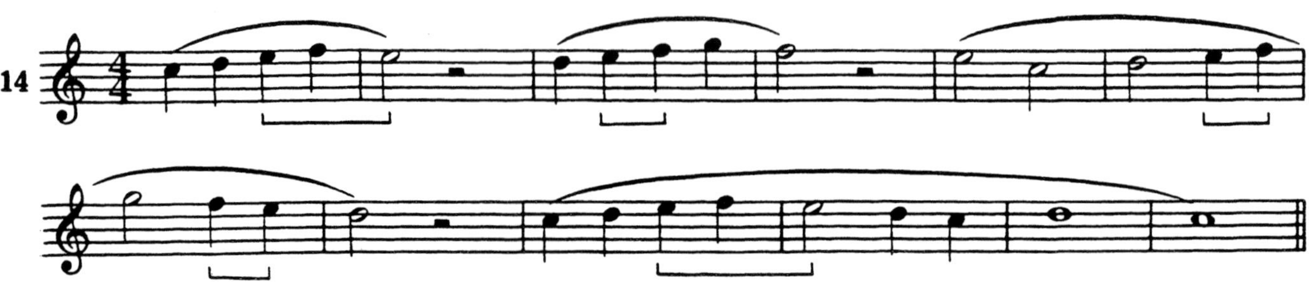

The movements of the tongue and of the fingers have so far been considered independently. In the following exercises they are combined. The action of the tongue should be exactly as in Exercises 1 – 5, the finger movements coinciding exactly with the pronunciation of the consonant 'D'. Cross fingerings are easier when the notes are tongued as the tiny separation between the notes is sufficient to cover any slight lack of synchronization in the finger movements, but avoid the temptation to lengthen the separation merely to disguise poor fingering.

EXERCISES

Tongue every note. Exercises 6 – 16 can also be practised tongued.

19

20

21

Slurring and tonguing combined

(c) Fingering with both hands

EXERCISES

Exercise 25 should be practised very slowly. Make sure that as finger 6 is lowered to produce the note G fingers 4 and 5 stay firmly covering their holes, and that as finger 7 is lowered for the F finger 6 keeps its position. Most beginners find the bottom note difficult: the little finger which is so much shorter than the others has usually to be stretched to reach the bottom hole and this causes its neighbour to be pulled away from its correct position. On most recorders the foot joint can be adjusted to suit individual players.

Remember that the breath pressure for the low notes should remain firm.

When playing a bottom F after a C or other note fingered with the left hand alone it is possible to place finger 7 on its hole while the higher note is still sounding. Exercise 27 demonstrates this technique; finger 7 can remain in position the whole time. The stabilizing finger is sometimes referred to as the *buttress finger*.

On most recorders this principle may be applied to the low F sharp, G and G sharp. In Exercises 28 – 44 a half bracket (⌈) over a note indicates that while that note is sounding the *lowest* finger required for the *subsequent* note may be lowered in preparation. The use of the buttress finger for support wherever possible, irrespective of the subsequent note, has some historical validity (see Part II, Section 2) but in the early stages of playing the technique should be confined to the usage described here.

Exercises 30 – 44 employ all the notes of the first register and are designed to provide a firm foundation for finger technique. They are short and simple in musical content, but should be practised slowly and carefully, aiming for good synchronization of tongue and fingers, rhythmic accuracy and above all, firm, well-supported tone.

Alternative E

Alternative fingerings are discussed in Section 8, but the commonest of them, 0 - 2 3 - - - - for E, may be used in Exercises 31, 41 and 42 for notes marked with a cross (x). It facilitates legato movement between E and C, F′ or G′.

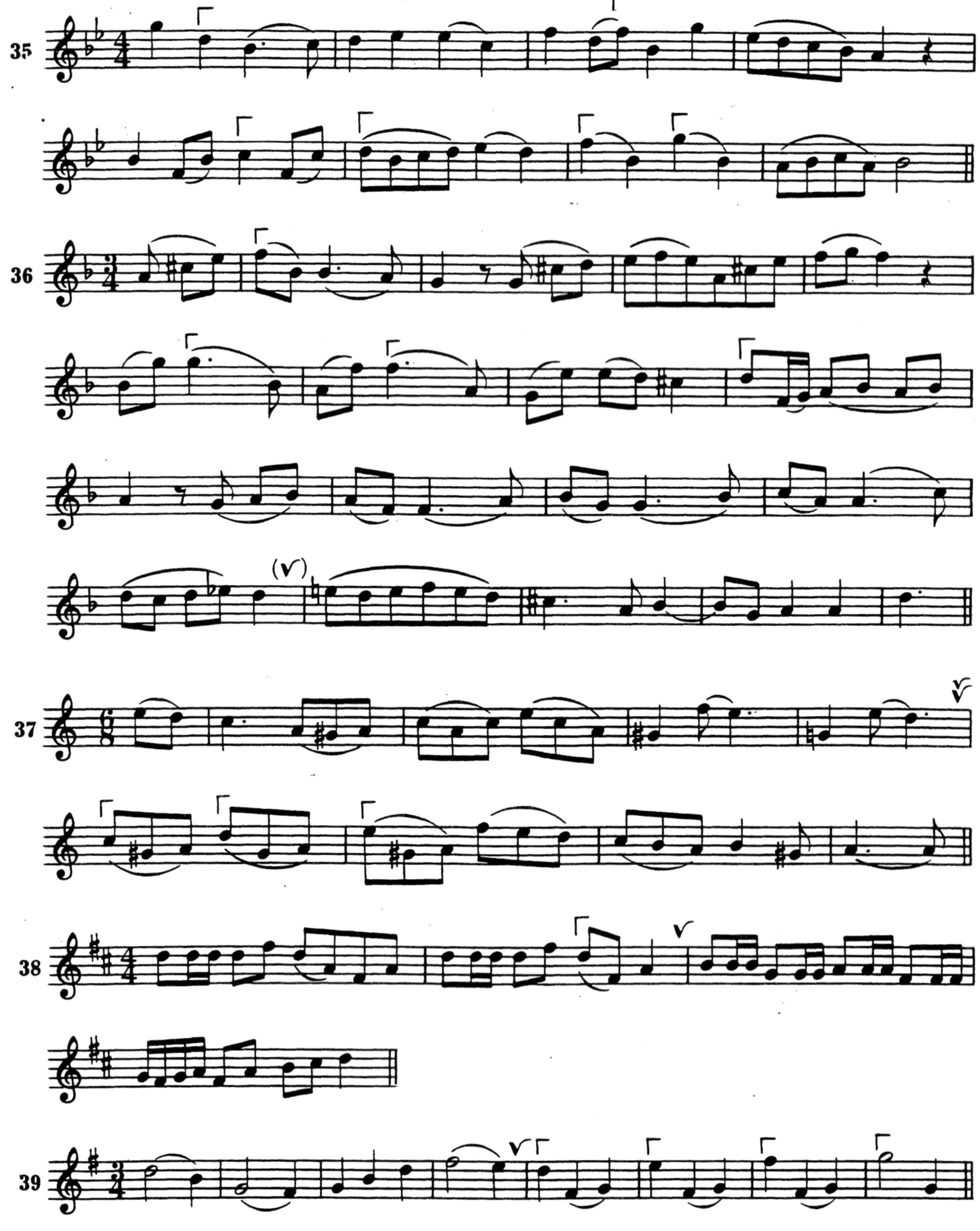
35
36
37
38
39

40

41

42

43
poco rall.
a tempo
44

4 The second register

All the notes above G′ sharp are played with the thumb-hole partly open. Play the note C and without moving any other fingers, bend the thumb-joint to form a small opening between the thumb-nail and the edge of the hole, increasing the breath pressure at the same time. This should produce the upper C′. Notes produced in this way are sometimes referred to as 'pinched' notes.

Remember the following points:

i) The size of opening in the thumb-hole must be governed by the *thumb-nail*, not the ball of the thumb.

ii) Correct thumbing will be impossible if the nail is too long, too short, uneven or broken.

iii) When changing from a note in the first register to a 'pinched' note, the thumb movement should be as small as possible. It is never necessary to do more than bend the joint slightly to bring the nail correctly into position.

iv) The amount of increase in breath pressure necessary for the second register must be discovered by trial and error; with experience the adjustment of breath when changing registers should become unconscious.

EXERCISES

The notes C′, A′ and D′ are all played with the same fingerings as the lower octave plus the partly open thumb-hole. Exercise 45 should be practised with and without the slurs and with particular attention to intonation.

48
49
50

The upper B′ and B′ flat require one finger less and the upper C′ sharp two fingers less than their first register equivalents (see fingering chart in Section 1).

EXERCISES

54

55

5 The third and fourth registers

The three notes of the third register, E′ flat, E′ and F″, must be blown more strongly than the second register. They may also vary in their response to the tongue, and to sound well in tune may need small adjustments to the size of the thumb-hole aperture, so that familiarity with the characteristics of individual instruments is most important. However, the following points will apply to the majority of recorders:

i) A cold recorder will collect condensation in the windway which will impair the tone quality of all the notes and make the high ones almost impossible. Always warm a recorder by blowing down it before playing, and before playing a passage involving high notes take particular care to ensure that the instrument is free from excess moisture. In an emergency a sharp intake of breath through the instrument will often clear it; when more time is available remove the moisture by shaking the head joint sharply or by carefully inserting a feather (a pheasant feather is best) down the windway.

ii) E′ flat speaks easily on most recorders with moderate tonguing and thumbing.

iii) E′ requires fairly strong tonguing and wide thumbing to sound in tune. Many recorders will only speak on this note if the thumbing is very close, causing flatness. This must be corrected by widening the thumbing as soon as the note has spoken.

iv) F″ requires close thumbing and slightly softer tonguing than E′.

v) Since the tonguing is so important in producing these high notes it follows that legato passages are often difficult if not impossible at this altitude. Experience will best reveal what can safely be attempted. Most of the slurs in the following exercises will give little trouble; all are possible with practice.

EXERCISES

58

59

G″ is the only note in the fourth register generally acknowledged as part of the normal compass. It speaks easily on most recorders with strong breath pressure, medium thumbing and fairly strong tonguing. Ø 1 - 3 4 - - 7 sometimes is preferable to the standard fingering.

Of the other possible notes in the fourth register, the most useful are G″ sharp, A″ and C″. All require strong breath pressure, close thumbing and strong tonguing. They cannot be played quietly!

G″ sharp (A″ flat)

0 1 - 3 - - - -
Ø - 2 3 - 5 6 -

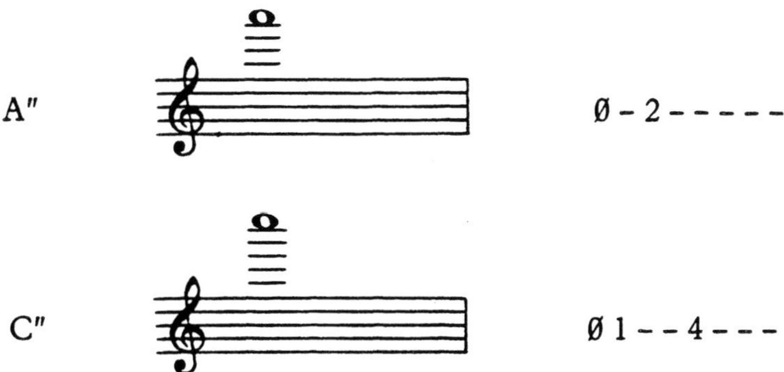

F″ sharp has always been a problem. Although it occurs in genuine recorder music it cannot be produced in any way that is completely satisfactory. There are four possibilities:

i)	Ø - - - 4 5 - -	This can only be used if the F″ sharp is slurred from an E′ or F″.
ii)	Ø 1 2̸ 3 4 5 6 7	2 should be only slightly open. This fingering produces a note of poor tone quality on many instruments.
iii)	Ø 1 2 3 4 5 6̸ 7	Variable in quality, and a little uncomfortable.
iv)	Ø 1 - 3 4 - 6 - K	K indicates stopping the end of the recorder with the knee, or by means of a bell key. This method produces a good note, clear and well in tune.

EXERCISES

61
Fine
D.C. al Fine
62
63

6 Articulation

The normal method of articulation is that described in Section 3(a). A small separation is made between the notes by the action of the tongue on the ridge behind the upper front teeth, as though pronouncing the consonant 'D'. Although this action is usually made as lightly as possible, it is sometimes musically desirable to increase the force within certain limits, so that one may conveniently refer to 'soft tonguing' and 'hard tonguing'. In addition the length of separation between the notes may be increased to produce 'short tonguing' as opposed to the more usual 'long tonguing'. Thus four basic permutations are possible with many shades of variety between them, but remember that the length of the notes may be varied much more than the force of the tongue strokes. Tonguing too hard is a very common fault among amateur recorder players.

65
66
67

Subtle variety in articulation is one of the most important means of expression on the recorder, whose dynamic range is naturally limited. In particular, a convincing echo effect can be produced by the use of lightly tongued staccato.

Double tonguing

When a passage of tongued notes has to be played quickly, single tonguing, the method of articulation so far described, becomes impracticable. The capability of individual players to produce a light, even articulation at speed using single tonguing varies greatly, but it would be true to say that for every player there is a crucial speed at which it becomes impossible to single tongue without stiffening the tongue and emphasizing its movement, thereby producing an undesirable hardness in the articulation or even an unpleasant spluttering effect. It then becomes necessary to resort to double tonguing.

Double tonguing is a method of articulation which divides the muscular effort between the tip and the slightly less sensitive, middle part of the tongue—as though saying 'D - G - D - G'. This should be tried at first on a single note and then on a simple scale passage, taking care to synchronize the double action of the tongue with the movements of the fingers.

EXERCISES

Repeat Exercises 70 and 71 on all notes.

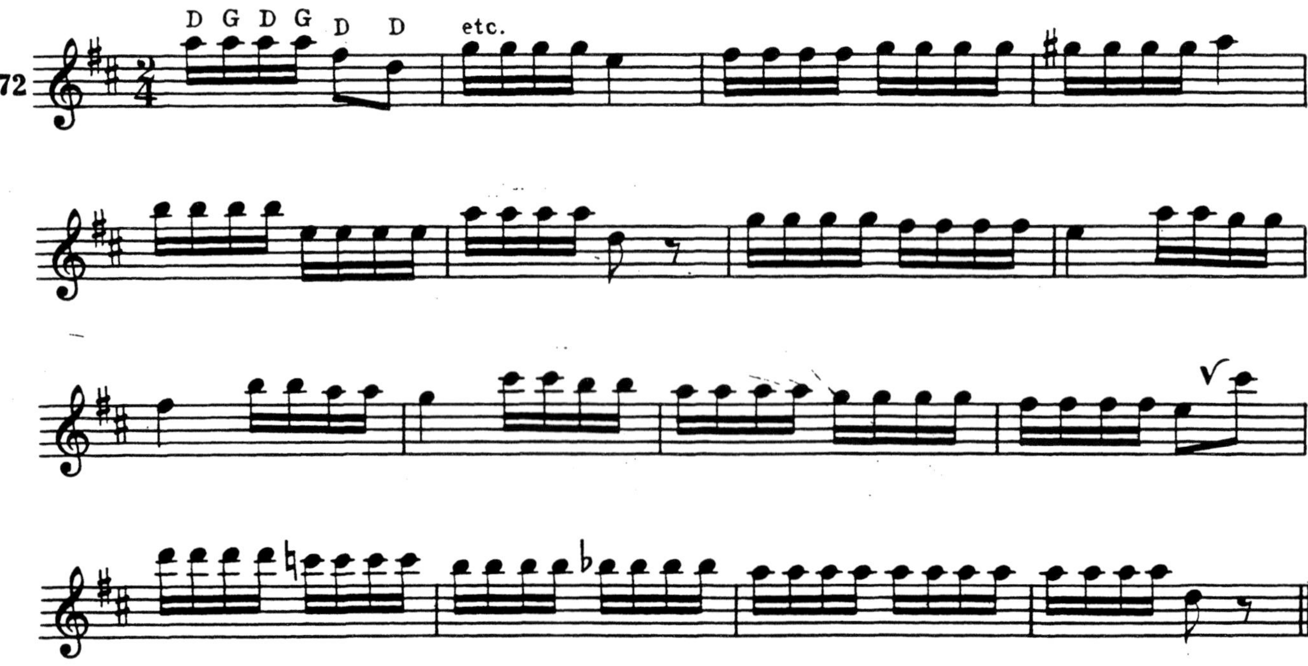

In the seventeenth and eighteenth centuries woodwind players used methods of double tonguing which exploited the inequality of a variety of consonants, and this historical aspect of articulation is discussed in Part II. The modern technique of double tonguing aims ideally to produce a uniform attack and notes of equal length. In practice, however, it is virtually impossible to prevent the 'D' consonant from sounding slightly stronger than the 'G', so that a passage of double tonguing beginning on an upbeat should always begin with the 'G' consonant.

76 D D G D D G D G

D G

Triple tonguing

Triplets or passages in fast compound time can be played with triple tonguing using the consonants 'D - G - D' or, to soften the attack on the third note in each group, 'D - G - L' or 'D - G - R'.

77 

Staccato

Staccato playing is usually better achieved with single tonguing than with double or triple tonguing. A true staccato involves the shortening of a note or group of notes *without necessarily altering the strength of articulation*. Each note is made measurably shorter than its written value — a sound followed by a silence all within the written value of the note. It follows that the stopping of the note with the tongue is just as important as the beginning so that single tonguing, in which only the sensitive tip of the tongue is used, produces the most satisfactory staccato. Double or triple tonguing need only be used for fast passages.

7 Vibrato

Vibrato is the deliberate and regular distortion of pitch for the purpose of enlivening tone quality. It is used by string, brass and woodwind players and singers and can be produced in a variety of ways. It should be a part of every recorder player's technique, but a true, deliberate vibrato should not be confused with the uncontrolled waver in the tone which is produced by many beginners. It is most unwise to attempt to use vibrato on the recorder until one is able to play long sustained notes with a completely even tone throughout the compass of the instrument.

There are two generally recognized ways of producing vibrato on the recorder:

(a) Throat vibrato

This is produced by using the back of the throat as a valve which partially restricts the flow of air, as though one were saying very softly 'ha-ha-ha-ha'. Throat vibrato is a relatively easy technique to acquire but can be difficult to control. It can easily degenerate into an unpleasant bleating sound unless great care is exercised.

(b) Diaphragm vibrato

This is produced by regulating the air flow from its source, the diaphragm, so that by the time it passes into the instrument the fluctuations in pressure which cause the alterations in pitch are well under control. Diaphragm vibrato is more difficult to produce than throat vibrato but has a less distorting effect on the general tone quality and once mastered is easier to control.

The extent of pitch distortion, which should be to both sides of the note, will usually vary in inverse proportion to the speed of the fluctuations, whether produced from the diaphragm or the throat. It is best to begin practising vibrato on long notes, making the fluctuations as slow and wide as possible. On a good recorder it is possible to vary the pitch by as much as a semitone on either side of the note. In this way it is easy to feel and hear exactly what is happening. The speed can gradually increase, so that it becomes possible to play any note on the recorder with varying degrees of vibrato.

EXERCISES

The vibrato is shown diagramatically by a wavy line. These preliminary exercises should be practised on all notes.

80 *a)*

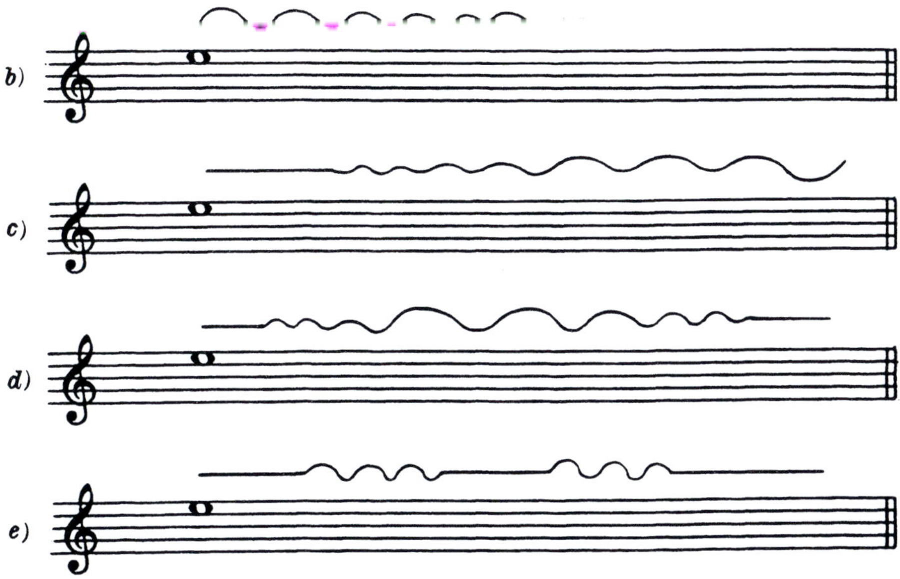

The extent to which vibrato may be used in any specific musical context is a matter of aesthetic judgement rather than technique and is therefore outside the scope of this book, but it should always be used to some musical purpose and never merely from habit.

Exercise 81 should be practised with various degrees of vibrato on the notes marked ∿∿ . Many of the previous exercises may also be practised in the same way.

8 Alternative fingerings, sliding and shading

Nearly every note on the recorder can be produced by using at least one fingering other than the standard one, and alternative fingerings provide a most valuable extension of recorder technique. All alternative fingerings are forked; the alternative for a note whose standard fingering is already forked will be a more extreme fork (E flat, for example, has as one of its alternatives 0 – 2 3 4 – (6) –) so that the tone quality of a note produced with an alternative fingering will usually be inferior to that produced by the standard fingering. The art of using alternative fingerings depends, therefore, on the ability to decide whether any deficiencies in tone quality or intonation are sufficiently offset by the various advantages about to be discussed to justify the use of alternative fingerings in any given context.

Trills

The most important use of alternative fingerings is in playing those trills which would be very impractical if not impossible with the standard fingerings. The speed of execution which is proper to a trill is usually sufficient to disguise any defect in tone or intonation caused by the alternative fingerings, but if a trill begins on the upper note (as in most baroque music it should) and the upper note is to be fingered during the trill with an alternative, the initial upper note, which will form an appoggiatura, should be played with the standard fingering to ensure good tone and intonation. The trill proper, which is in effect a decorated resolution of the appoggiatura, can then be fingered with the alternative. This is demonstrated in exercise 82. Trilling fingers are marked with an asterisk (*).

Written A: Ø 1 2 3 4 5 – –
G/A trill: – 1 2 3 4 5* 6 7

If a trill ends with a turn, this can sometimes best be played by adding more fingers below the already forked main note, as in exercise 83.

Written F: 0 – 2 – – – – –
E/F trill: 0 – 2 3* – – – –
D in turn: 0 – 2 3 4 5 – – (blow softly)
Final D: 0 1 2 – – – – –

The following table of trill fingerings covers all trills which cannot be played with standard fingerings with the exception of the low F/F sharp trill which is impossible.

	$0\ 1\ 2\ 3\ 4\ 5\ \overset{\star}{6}\ \not{7}$	G sharp is sharp
	$0\ 1\ 2\ 3\ 4\ 5\ \not{6}\ \overset{\star}{7}$	
	$0\ 1\ 2\ 3\ 4\ \overset{\star}{5}\ \not{6}\ -$	B flat is slightly sharp
	$0\ 1\ 2\ 3\ 4\ \overset{\star}{5}\ -\ -$	B flat is sharp
	$0\ 1\ 2\ 3\ \overset{\star}{4}\ 5\ -\ -$	B is sharp
	$0\ 1\ 2\ 3\ 4\ -\ \overset{\star}{6}\ \overset{\star}{7}$	
	$0\ 1\ 2\ 3\ \overset{\star}{4}\ -\ 6\ 7$	
	$0\ 1\ 2\ \overset{\star}{3}\ -\ 5\ 6\ 7$	C sharp is sharp

0 1 2 - 4 5 6 7
0 1 - 3 4 5 6 7
0 1 - 3 4 5 6 -
0 1 - 3 4 - - -
0 - 2 3 4 - - -
0 1 - 3 4 - - -
- 1 2 3 4 5 - -
0 - 2 3 - - - -
0 1 - - - - - -
- 1 2 3 4 - - -
0 - 2 - - - - -
- 1 2 3 - - - -
- 1 - 3 4 5 6 -
- 1 2 3 4 5 6 7
- 1 2 3 4 5 6 7
- - 2 3 4 5 6 -
- - 2 3 4 5 6 -
Ø 1 2 3 4 5 6 -
Ø 1 2 3 4 - 6 7
Ø 1 2 3 4 5 - - B flat is sharp
Ø 1 2 3 - 5 6 -
Ø 1 2 3 4 - 6 -
Ø 1 2 3 - 5 - -
Ø 1 2 - 4 - 6 -

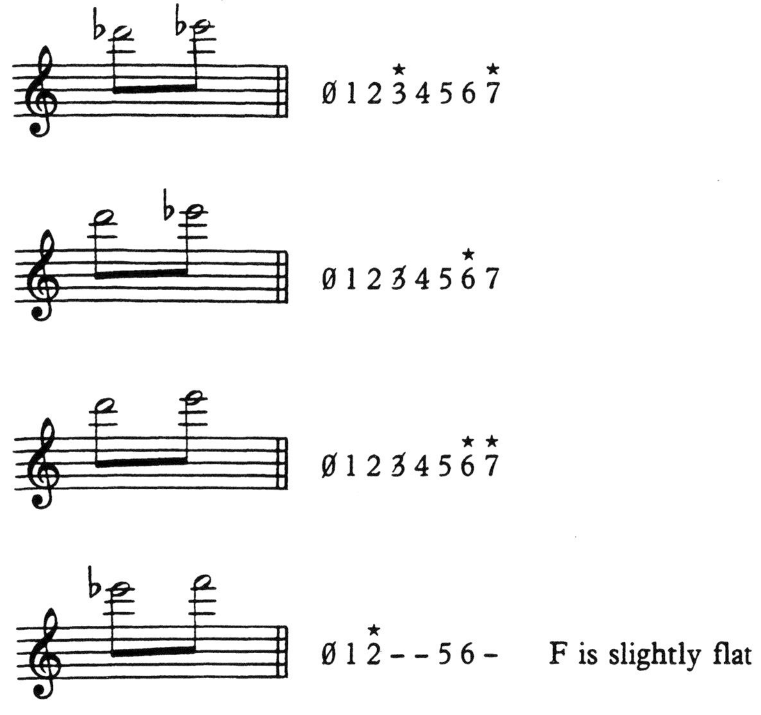

EXERCISES

85

The use of alternative fingerings is by no means limited to trills. Further uses include passage work, legato groupings, dynamic and tonal variation and intonation control.

Passage work

Difficult passages can often be made easier by using alternative fingerings which reduce the amount of finger movement. Apart from the well-known alternative E (0 – 2 3 – – – –) particularly useful alternatives for passage work are the following:

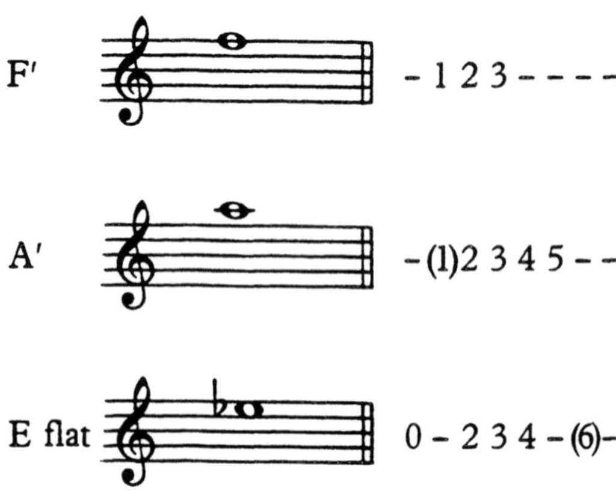

The alternative fingering for A′ produces a good clear note virtually indistinguishable from that produced with the standard fingering. The alternative fingering can be converted to standard fingering after the note has been sounded by placing the thumb-nail correctly in position on the thumb-hole with no noticeable alteration in pitch or tone quality.

In exercise 87 and subsequent exercises, use the appropriate alternative fingerings for notes marked x. Begin the A′ in the second bar of exercise 87 with the alternative fingering, then change to the standard in preparation for high C′. Do the reverse in the third bar.

Legato groupings

The alternative fingerings used for trills can also be effective in some legato passages which include step-wise movement. In exercise 89 alternatives should be used only on notes marked ×. Except where otherwise marked, the fingerings to be used are to be found in the table of trill fingerings.

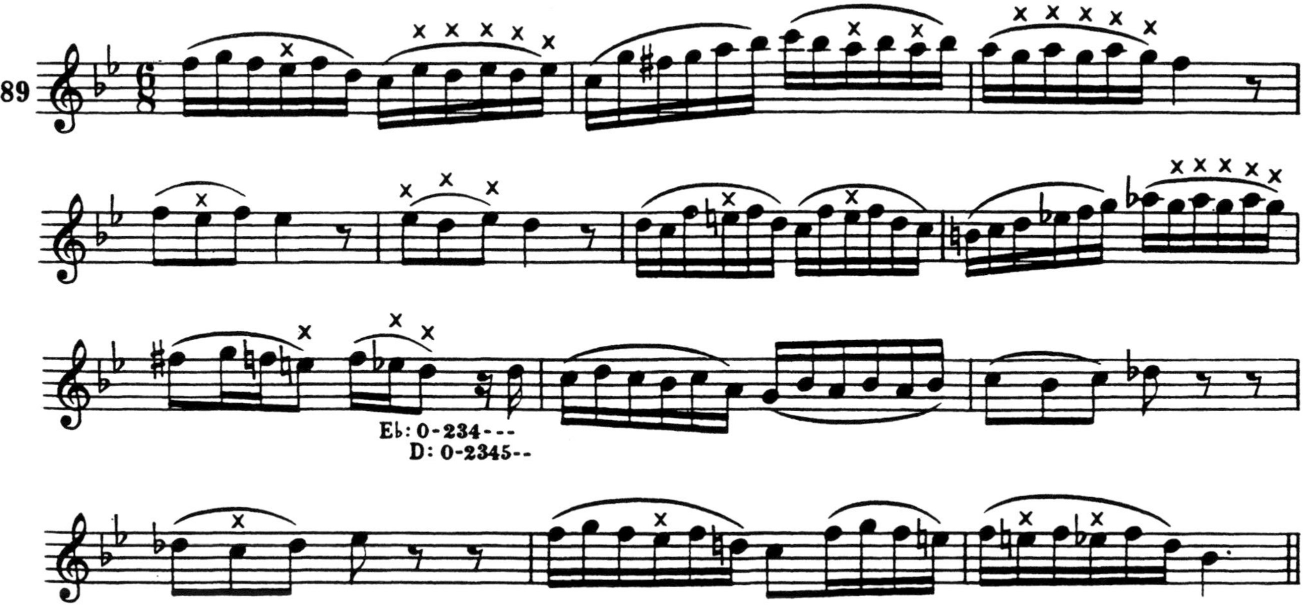

Dynamic and tonal variation and intonation control

The same trill/legato fingerings, being forked, are weaker in tone than the standard fingerings and can be used to shape phrase endings by suggesting a diminuendo effect.

Further dynamic variation can be obtained by deliberately choosing out-of-tune fingerings and correcting the pitch by an increase or decrease in breath pressure producing a corresponding change in volume. An exhaustive study of alternative fingerings is beyond the scope of this book; indeed the possibilities are infinite, and serious players will discover for themselves the capabilities of their instrument as need and opportunity arise.

The modification of both standard and alternative fingerings by slightly opening a stopped hole to produce sharpness (sliding) and partially restricting the flow of air from an open hole (shading) provides still further scope for dynamic variation.

Slide fingering

There are two possible methods of slide fingering. The finger can either be drawn away from the hole to form a small opening between the tip of the finger and the edge of the hole, or it can be pushed across the hole so that air escapes from the opposite side (see illustration). Slide fingering is effective with most forked fingerings but produces extreme sharpness when applied to plain fingered notes.

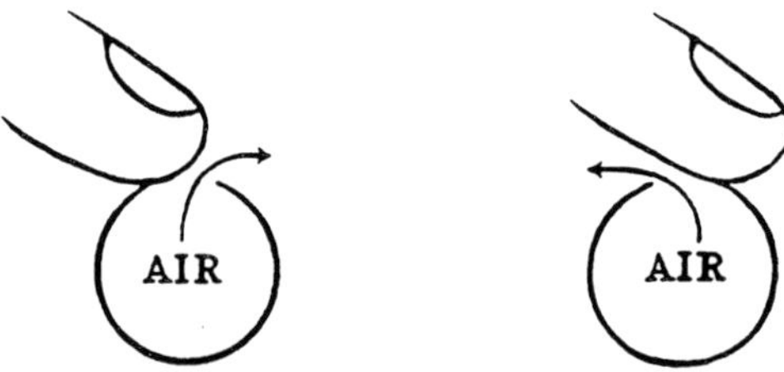

Two methods of slide fingering

Shading

Any note other than bottom F can be flattened by shading, though for notes above C″ close thumbing is a more satisfactory method of flattening. Shading fingers are either held over one or more of the open holes at a distance of anything between a sixteenth and a quarter of an inch (the closer the flatter) or placed on the edge of the hole (see illustration).

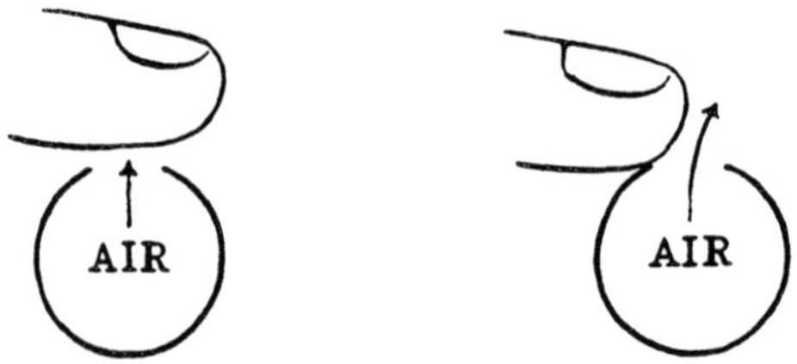

Two methods of shading

Shading is a relatively easy technique to acquire and should become automatic as a means of controlling pitch and volume. Slide fingering should be approached more cautiously. With practice it is possible by means of careful co-ordination of breath control, shading and slide fingering to obtain a fairly wide range of crescendo and diminuendo effects.

9 Scales and arpeggios

In these arrangements of the scales and arpeggios for the treble recorder, the following principles have been adopted.

(a) Range

The only scales which can be played complete through two octaves on the treble recorder are F and A flat major, the two forms of F minor and the descending forms of A and G melodic minor. A few more arpeggios are available. In order to cover as much of the instrument's compass as possible, each scale or arpeggio begins on the key-note, ascends to the highest practical note (see (b) below), descends to the lowest practical note and returns to the key-note.

(b) Upper limits

The high A″ flat, A″ and C″ have been included but not the high F″ sharp. Where the highest available note in a scale was the seventh that scale has been taken only as far as the sixth.

(c) Exceptions

A few departures from (a) and (b) have been made for the sake of neatness and symmetry.

(d) Articulations

No articulation marks have been given. Practising scales and arpeggios slurred is an excellent way of finding out faults in fingering, but a few high notes will not speak unless tongued. These have been marked with the letter T. This letter in brackets indicates that the note *may* have to be tongued. Scales and arpeggios should also be practised using various methods of tonguing – single and double, hard and soft, long and short – and with varied combinations of tonguing and slurring.

C major

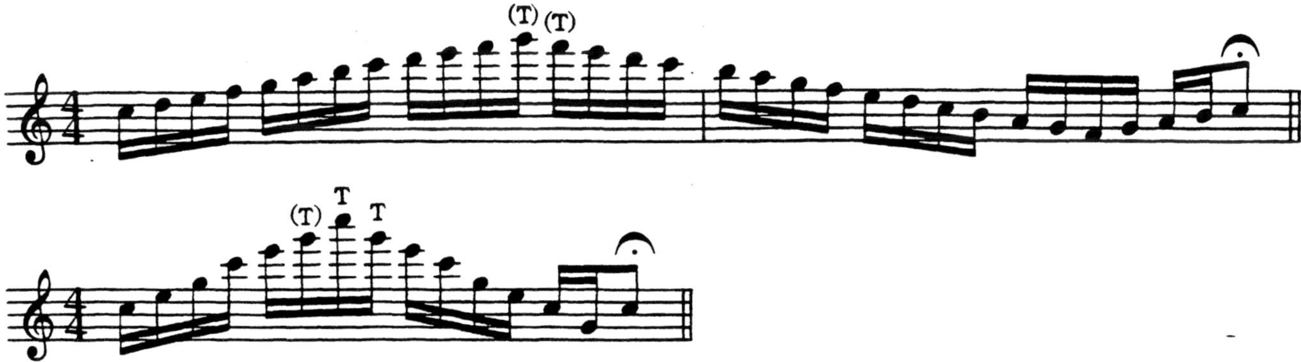

A minor

T

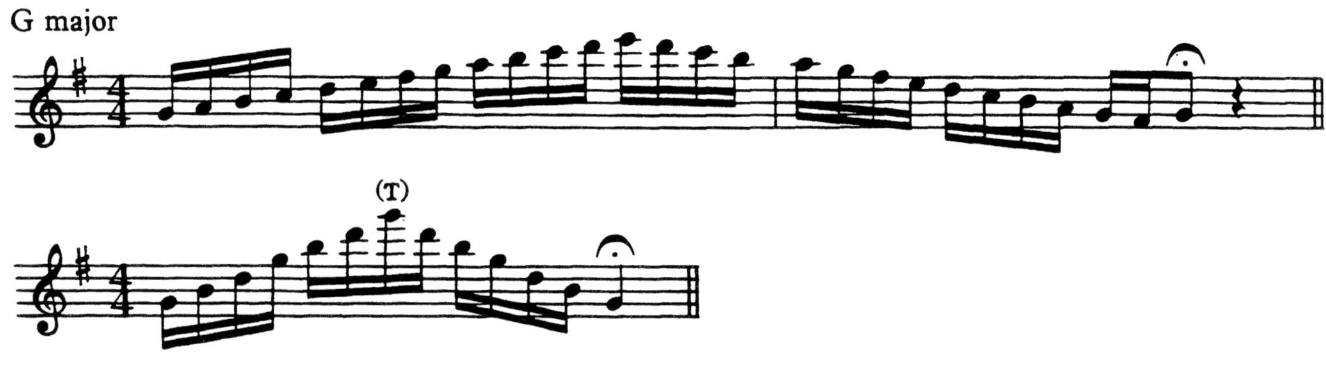
G major
(T)

E minor
(T)

F major
(T)
(T)
(T)
(T)
D minor
(T)(T)
(T)(T)
T (T)
D major
B minor

B flat major
(T)
(T)
G minor
(T)
A major
F sharp minor

E flat major
(T)
(T)
C minor
(T)
(T)
(T)
(T)
(T)
T
(T)
E major
C sharp minor
(T)
(T)
(T)

A flat major
F minor
B major
G sharp minor

D flat major
(T)
(T)
(T)
B flat minor
(T)
(T)
F sharp major
(T)
E flat minor
(T)

Dominant Seventh Arpeggios

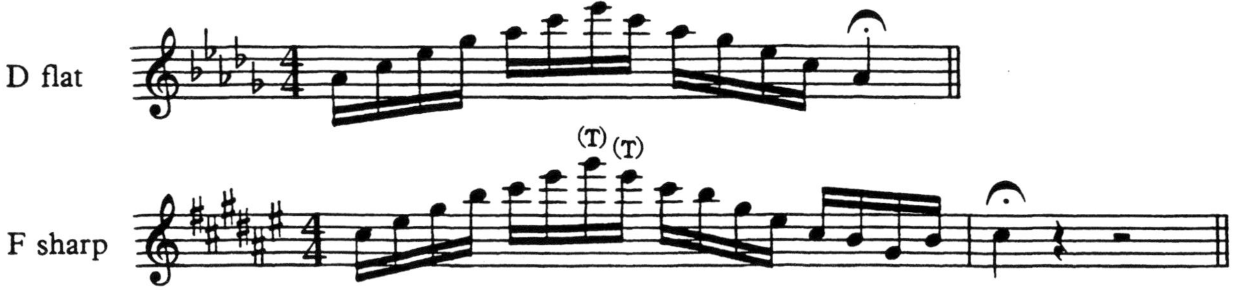

Diminished Seventh Arpeggios

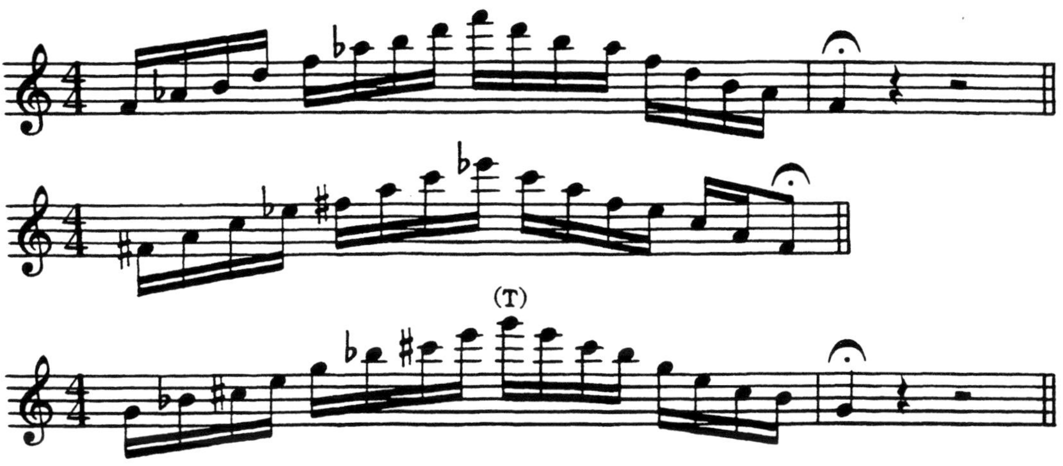

The Chromatic Scale

Short chromatic scale passages are often best played with some alternative fingerings, but it is still useful to practise the complete chromatic scale as given below with the standard fingerings.

10 Technical studies

1

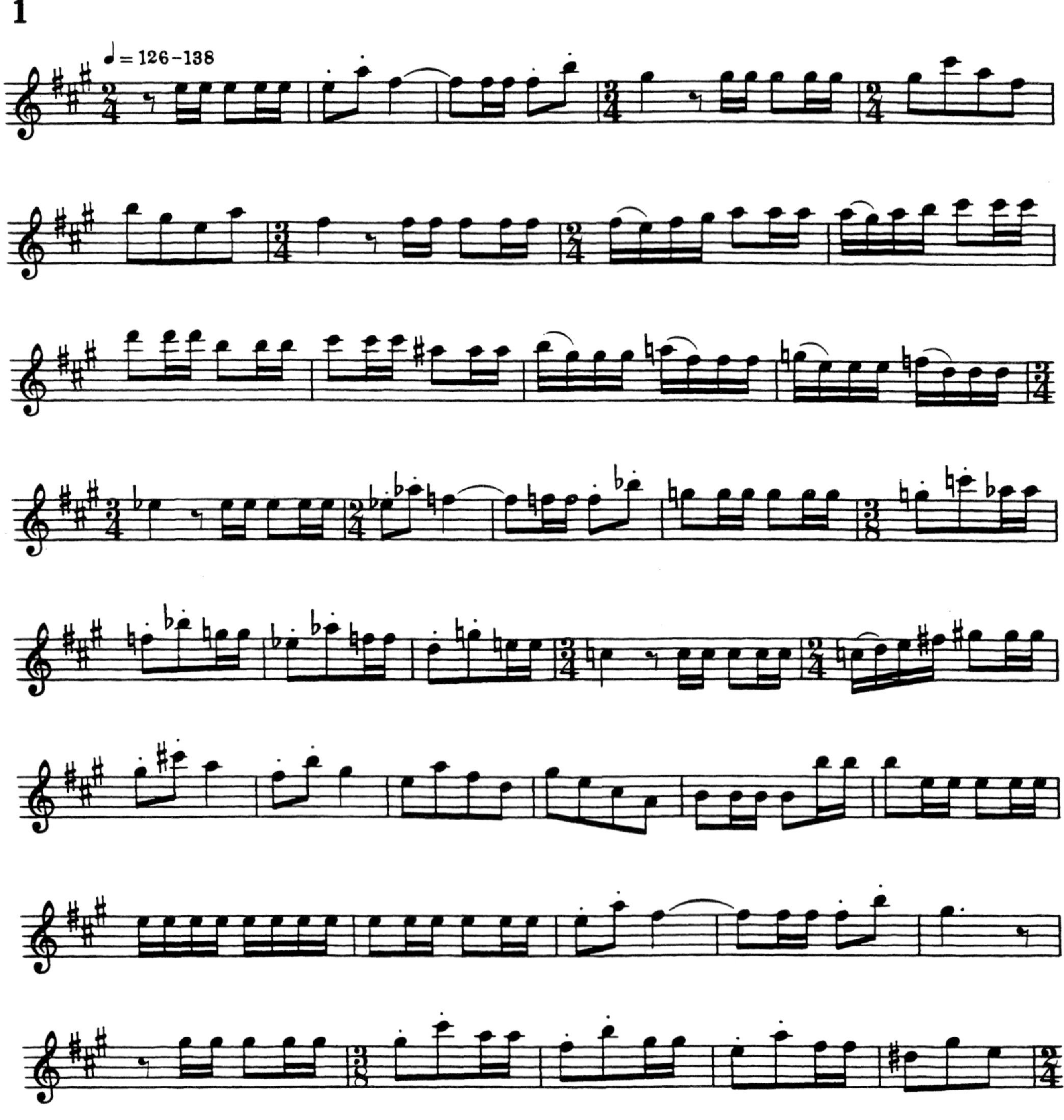

2
♩ = 48 – 52
3
3

3

4
𝅗𝅥 = 112 – 120

5

♩ = 72 – 80

6

♩ = 88 – 96

7
♩ = 116 – 126

PART II

1 Repertoire and style

The Middle Ages and Renaissance

The Middle Ages

In recent years there has been an extraordinary upsurge of interest in medieval music among performers and listeners as opposed to scholars and musicologists. However, our knowledge of musical performance practice before about 1400 is very limited, and those who specialize in performing medieval music would be the first to admit that their efforts are based largely on informed speculation. One problem for the recorder player is that there are no surviving instruments from that period. Iconographic evidence suggests that recorders have existed since the thirteenth century, but we have no real information about the instruments or exactly what music they played. There would seem to be no reason why recorder players should not appropriate any medieval music, either instrumental or vocal, which suits their instrument provided that no claim is made to an authentic medieval repertoire for the recorder. Most of the published medieval music is in collected editions or anthologies rather than in editions intended for practical use, and as hardly any music of this period was intended for a specified instrumental combination there is considerable scope for the imaginative arranger.

A few recorder makers are now producing instruments based on the little evidence we have about recorders in the middle ages.

The Renaissance

I Repertoire

By its very nature, cultural activity in the Renaissance was better documented than that of the Middle Ages. Musical instruments of all kinds, including recorders, survive in substantial numbers, and contemporary accounts of musical performances reveal interesting details of the ways in which instruments were used. Recorders were used both in sacred and secular contexts, usually in homogeneous consorts, either to double or alternate with voices, or to play instrumental music in their own right. It is no more possible with renaissance music than with medieval music to identify a specific recorder repertoire, but one can be sure that recorder playing, especially in Italy, was developed to an advanced degree of virtuosity.

Instrumental ensemble music, especially the more serious fantasias and *In Nomines*, was intended primarily for viols, but can equally well be played on wind instruments, or by a mixed group of wind and strings, and a large quantity of such music has been published in editions made specifically for recorders. Recorders can combine successfully, if not particularly authentically, with enclosed reed instruments such as the crumhorn in dance music. The standard 'broken consort' of three plucked instruments, two viols, and a recorder or flute was a sophisticated ensemble which became fashionable in England towards the end of the sixteenth century.

In addition to music published in recorder editions, collected editions and anthologies offer recorder players a useful source of material. The following are all worth investigating:

MORLEY, THOMAS — First Book of Consort Lessons (Peters) (arrangements of dances and popular songs for 'broken consort' by Morley and his contemporaries)

MUSICA BRITTANICA (Stainer & Bell)

Volume 1	Medieval Carols
Volume 8	Complete Works of John Dunstable
Volume 9	Jacobean Consort Music
Volume 15	Music of Scotland, 1500–1700
Volume 18	Music at the Court of Henry VIII

II Style

(a) Instruments

Although renaissance music has for many years formed the staple diet of most amateur recorder ensembles, it is only in relatively recent times that there has been much interest in the kind of recorders which would have been played in the sixteenth and early seventeenth centuries. There is no doubt, however, that recorders modelled on renaissance originals produce a far more satisfying sound in music of that period than do modern instruments based loosely on baroque patterns. The renaissance recorder was an instrument of noble simplicity which had a wide, roughly cylindrical bore which favoured the lower register. Enough originals survive in good condition to enable makers to produce copies, but few of the originals are in a playable condition. Warping and shrinkage also make it difficult to determine accurately the pitch at which these instruments played, but it seems likely that the usual pitch for wind music was a little higher than the modern concert pitch (A440 Hz) which is adopted for most modern 'renaissance' recorders. A few specialist makers have taken A460 Hz as a standard pitch for renaissance wind instruments.

More important than the precise pitch of the renaissance recorder is the fact that the various sizes of instrument did not follow our familiar F and C spacing but were generally spaced a fifth apart. The standard recorder quartet consisted of a treble in G, two means (tenors) in C and a bass in F. Such a quartet could play most four-part vocal music in the written key sounding an octave higher at what we would now call 4′ pitch. By the early seventeenth century, this basic quartet had been extended upwards to include the descant in D and downwards to include the great bass in B flat. At this point, however, makers seem to have adopted a process of rationalization: the smallest recorder was made not in A which would be logical, but in G, an octave above the treble, which is practical. Similarly, the double bass was made in F, an octave below the normal bass. The existence of descants in C, tenors in D and basses in G suggests an attempt to carry the process of rationalization further towards the modern system, though curiously enough the one instrument for which there seems to be little evidence is the treble or alto in F which was to have its heyday less than a century later.

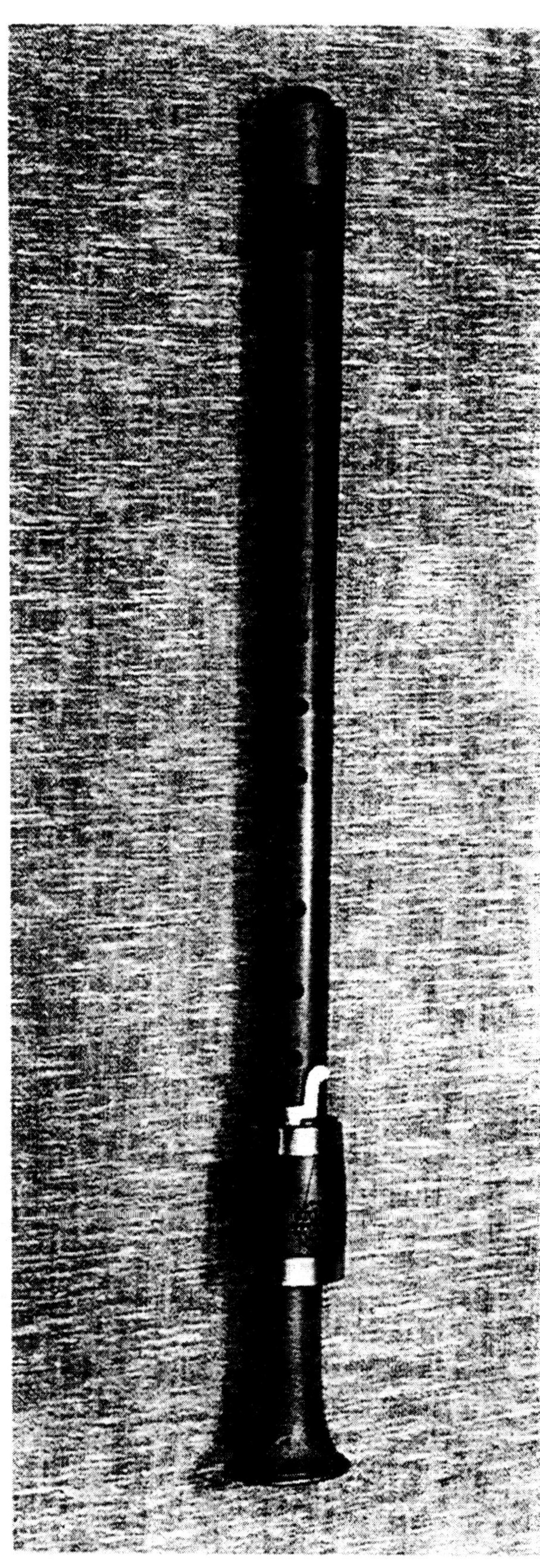

PLATE I: Bass recorder, Italian sixteenth century, in the Victoria and Albert Museum. The fontanelle which partly covers the key is a characteristic of the larger renaissance instruments.

(Photo: Victoria and Albert Museum) *Crown Copyright. Reproduced by permission*

(b) Performance technique

The earliest instruction book for the recorder, Sylvestro Ganassi's *Opera intitulata Fontegara*, published in Venice as early as 1535, suggests that, in Italy at least, recorder playing was developed to a fine art. Ganassi gives fingerings for a range of well over two octaves (see Section 2) as well as instructions for articulation and many examples of ornamentation. It seems likely, however, that few players would have aspired to the level of virtuosity implied by Ganassi, and that in the Renaissance the recorder was thought of principally as a consort instrument. The style of articulation and ornamentation appropriate to renaissance music are discussed in more detail in Sections 3 and 4, but a few general remarks on consort playing are included here.

Vibrato

Vibrato sounds anachronistic and should be avoided in renaissance consort music.

Ornamentation

Improvized ornamentation is more appropriate in dance music and light vocal music than in a complex contrapuntal texture, and in any music a good understanding between the members of the consort is necessary to produce an aesthetically satisfying result.

Articulation and dynamics

Many editions of recorder consort music contain anachronistic articulation and dynamic markings which must be disregarded. Strict observation of editorial slurs and staccato dots is likely to produce a fussy, unstylish performance. It is usually best to adopt a tongued legato as the basic articulation with the possibility of shortening certain notes to point the rhythm, characterize thematic material or simulate a dynamic contrast.

The Baroque Era

1 Repertoire

(a) The Early Baroque

During the first half of the seventeenth century there were important and far-reaching developments in music. This was the beginning of what we now call the 'baroque' era, the age of Monteverdi and early opera and the period in which an increasing polarization of melody and bass and a growing feeling for harmonic progression rapidly replaced the old contrapuntal style of the Renaissance. Instrumental music also flourished at this time, and although traces of the vocal style of the Renaissance remained, a distinct instrumental idiom emerged. Italian composers in particular exploited the expressive potential of a solo instrument with some form of accompaniment.

Though musical styles and fashions were changing and composers were becoming increasingly aware of the individual characteristics of particular instruments, there remained throughout the early baroque period a reluctance to commit a musical work to a particular instrumental sonority. This is to the recorder player's advantage, for many sonatas were written for a solo instrument ('canto solo') with continuo accompaniment. The most likely instruments the composers would have had in mind are the violin or the cornetto, but these sonatas fit very well the descant (soprano) recorder and provide a welcome addition to the repertoire of the recorder soloist. They are usually in one movement, but divided into sections of varying speeds and time-signatures. In addition to works such as these, *Der Fluyten Lust-hof*, a monumental collection of variations on different popular tunes of the time by the Flemish composer Jacob van Eyck, should be an indispensable part of every recorder player's library.

(b) The Late Baroque

From about 1680 to about 1730 was a Golden Age of solo recorder music. This was the period of supremacy of the treble (alto) recorder though the voice flute (alto in D) and sixth flute (soprano in D) were also widely used. The C recorders, our descant and tenor, were rarely used, though such instruments did exist. The repertoire is remarkably rich and includes not only sonatas, concertos and chamber music but also important parts in operas and orchestrally accompanied church music. A detailed account of the late baroque repertoire may be found in Edgar Hunt's book *The Recorder and its Music.*

The sonata repertoire is large and varied, including quite simple pieces probably intended for amateur performers as well as virtuoso works of formidable difficulty. There are also contemporary transcriptions of sonatas originally composed for other instruments, and upward transposition, usually of a minor third, of violin or flute music was a well-established practice. It is curious that recorder players today seem reluctant to take advantage of this convention of transposition as it makes available a large quantity of fine music with no loss of authenticity. It is very useful in this connection to be able to read the French violin clef (G on the bottom line) as this greatly facilitates the transposition of a third.

HANDEL Sonata in E minor, Opus 1, No. 1, for flute and continuo; first movement

Read as French violin clef or bass clef sounding two octaves higher, adjusting accidentals

sounds

If applied to a sixth flute or voice flute, fingering as a treble in F, this method of transposition makes flute and violin music available in the original key. The fact that many voice flutes survive from the baroque period suggests that this too may have been a common practice, though there is little documentary evidence to support such a theory. Exercises for transposition and reading the French violin clef may be found in Section 5.

In professional circles the recorder seems often to have been regarded as a doubling instrument and in many large-scale works by composers such as Handel and Purcell, a pair of recorders may replace the oboes for one or two items only. The same musicians would surely have played both instruments.

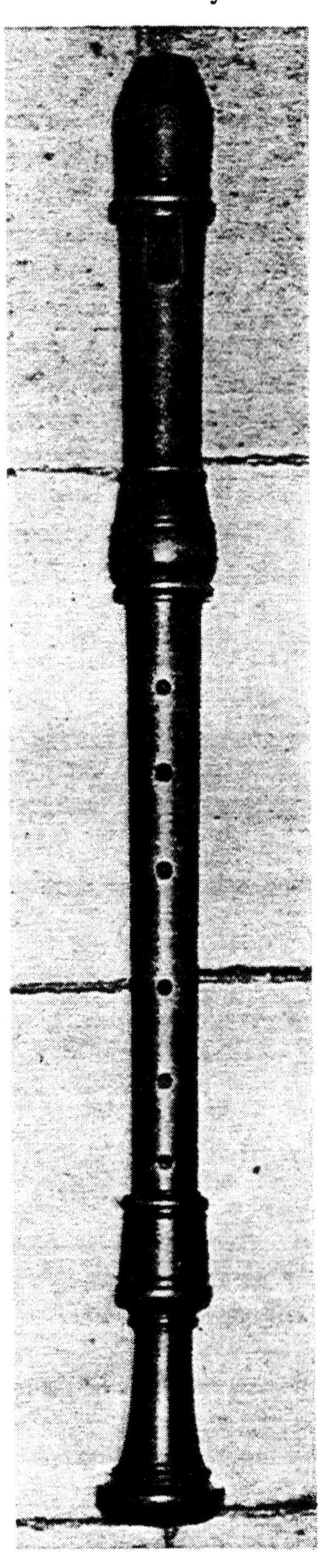

PLATE II: Voice flute by P.I.Bressan in Moyses Hall Museum, Bury St Edmunds

(Photo: Lewis Jones) *Reproduced by permission*

II Style

So large a proportion of the solo recorder repertoire consists of music from the late baroque period that a serious player of the instrument must be by definition a specialist with an interest in an authentic style of performance. The main sources of information on the stylized coventions of musical performance which evolved during the seventeenth and early eighteenth centuries are the instrumental tutors written by musicians of the period. Unfortunately they are often ambiguous and contradict one another, providing opportunities for endless scholarly arguments, but a number of basic principles do emerge fairly clearly and it is possible to evolve a tentative set of working rules. Individual problems can often be dealt with as they arise by reference to the standard authorities (see Section 7, 'Suggestions for further study'), but frequently there is no clear-cut solution and one must ultimately rely on common sense and sound musicianship.

(a) Instruments

It is possible to play a Handel recorder sonata using a Boehm flute and a grand piano. The result may sound very good and may even be said to have an authenticity of a kind, inasmuch as the use of modern instruments makes the music part of the living tradition of present-day performance practice. However, the character of the music of the past, even the relatively recent past, was determined to a large extent by the instruments which originally played it, and there is much to be gained from an attempt to use instruments, either originals or modern reconstructions, of the kind which existed when the music was written.

The modern recorder is based on the design of eighteenth-century instruments and compared with the flute and oboe has suffered very little obvious modernization. It is nevertheless essentially an all-purpose instrument, intended for playing modern music as well as the baroque repertoire, and certain important characteristics of the old recorders have been lost in the attempt by present-day makers to provide a really versatile modern instrument. Many performers now feel that in order to do full justice to the baroque repertoire it is necessary to play an original old instrument or at least a good, accurate copy. Genuine originals are of course scarce and command enormous prices on the open market, but there is a constantly increasing number of makers producing instruments modelled closely on specific originals or at least incorporating the important characteristics of the true baroque recorder.

During the first half of the seventeenth century the design of recorders remained much as it had been during the Renaissance, though some attempts were made to improve the high notes by narrowing the bore. This type of instrument is appropriate for the early Italian repertoire and composers such as Van Eyck, but the instrument known to Bach and Handel emerged from the experiments of French woodwind makers at some time in the second half of the seventeenth century, and surviving instruments in museums and private collections provide a variety of models for present-day makers. When buying a baroque recorder it is important to understand the characteristic features of the originals and to know whether the maker of the copy has incorporated them all or made some compromises. Compromises are not necessarily undesirable, but you should at least be aware of them. A true copy will have the following characteristics:

Voicing

The windway on old recorders is usually very narrow and often curved so that the instrument does not respond instantly to the breath; all but the shortest notes have a characteristic swell in the tone which cannot be reproduced on a modern instrument without an unacceptable distortion of the pitch.

Pitch

There was no absolute standard of pitch during the baroque period, but many surviving wind instruments play at a lower pitch than we are used to today. There are strong reasons for supposing that most baroque instrumental music should be played on instruments which sound at least a semitone below modern pitch.

Tuning and fingering

Modern wind instruments are made to sound in tune with a piano tuned in equal temperament. This method of tuning was unknown in the seventeenth and eighteenth centuries, though something like it was occasionally employed. The usual methods of tuning keyboard instruments were variants of meantone temperament in which major thirds of the more frequently used triads are made acoustically exact, that is to say, smaller than we are used to in equal temperament. The whole subject of early keyboard tunings and temperaments is a complex one which has not been fully researched, but it would seem that woodwind instruments were made to accord with some system of unequally tempered tuning. On a treble recorder, for example, the major third between C and E or between F and A would be appropriately small, and by using alternative fingerings a sharp could be made lower than its enharmonic flat. The fingerings of old recorders do not, therefore, always correspond to the established fingerings for the modern recorder as given in Part I. The fact that this standard modern fingering is sometimes referred to as 'baroque' fingering to distinguish it from the incorrect fingering system of some cheap German instruments only increases terminological confusion! It must be said that it is no easy matter to play regularly both on modern recorders and baroque recorders which require the old fingerings. It can be done, but at the risk of some deterioration in sight-reading ability. Section 2 contains a comparative chart of some of the more important early fingering systems.

It must not be assumed from what has been said above that modern recorders are quite unsuitable for baroque music. A good sense of style is more important than having exactly the right authentic instrument, and modern instruments may have certain practical advantages over their baroque ancestors, but when played skilfully and sympathetically old instruments can add an important dimension to our understanding of their music, and that is the real justification for playing them. Every recorder player should take advantage of any opportunity to play or hear old recorders.

PLATE III: *(opposite)* Baroque treble recorders in the Donaldson Collection, Royal College of Music.
Left to right:
Villars, French, late eighteenth century
J. W. Oberlender, Nuremberg, early eighteenth century
J. C. Denner, Nuremberg, early eighteenth century

(Photo: Royal College of Music) *Reproduced by permission*

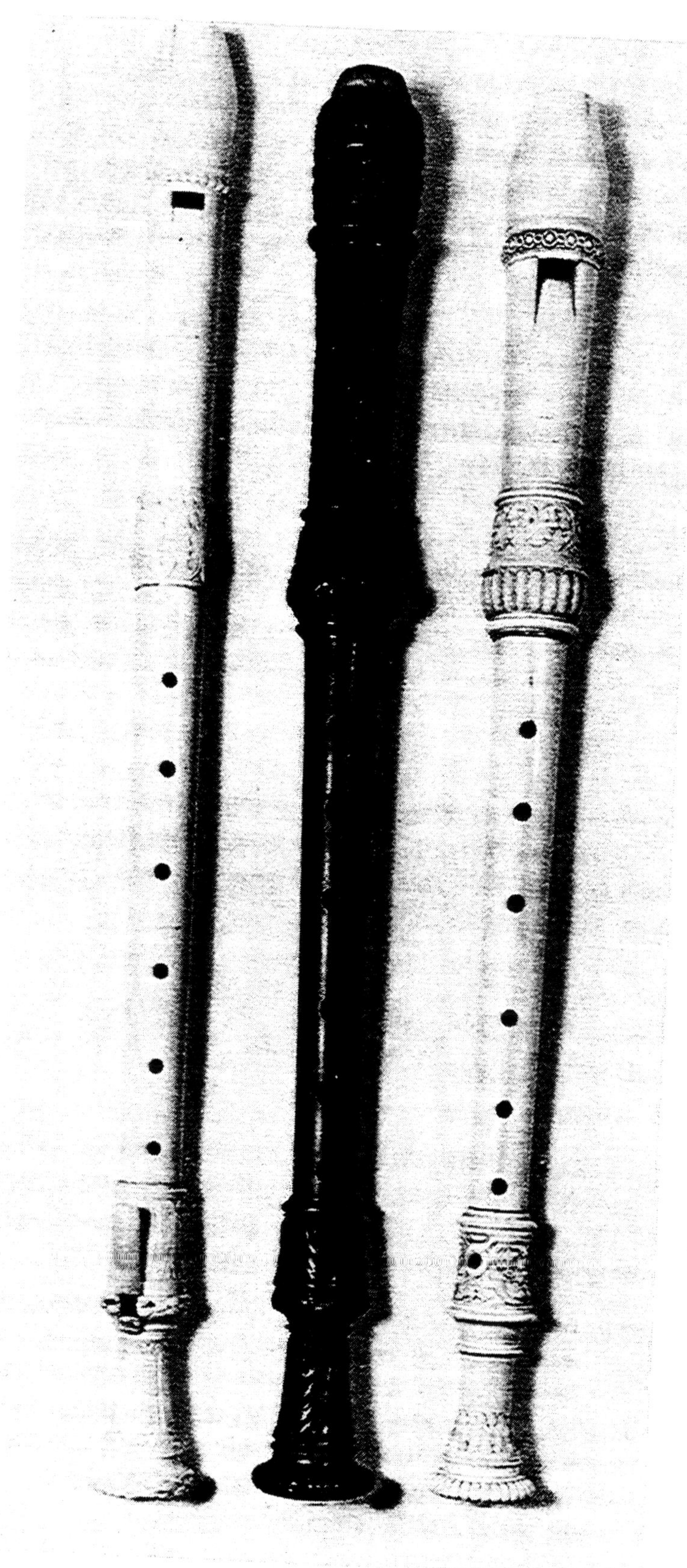

(b) Accompaniment

The keyboard accompanist in the seventeenth and eighteenth centuries was provided only with a copy of the bass line of a piece of music, the so-called basso continuo or thorough bass. Figures were usually added to the bass line to indicate to the player the harmonic progressions, and from this he would improvize a right-hand part, the left taking the original bass which might be doubled by a bass viol, cello or bassoon. The choice of keyboard instrument to accompany a recorder sonata may present something of a problem, availability being the largest factor. There are various possibilities:

Baroque harpsichord

The ideal instrument for most baroque accompaniment work is a seventeenth-century Italian-style harpsichord with two coupled 8′ stops. Original instruments in working order are rare, but good copies of Italian harpsichords and other baroque originals are easily available, though expensive. Many makers will also supply harpsichords in kit form.

Modern harpsichord

Much the same applies to the modern harpsichord as to the modern recorder. Most modern harpsichords are heavily built and have a variety of alternative registrations, usually pedal operated, to compensate for their lack of tonal brilliance. For continuo work the best effect is obtained by using a single 8′ stop or two coupled 8′ stops. 16′ and 4′ stops should not be used, and the registration should not be altered in the course of a movement.

Piano

The use of the piano for continuo accompaniment is of course anachronistic but if done with taste and discretion can be at least as acceptable as a big modern harpsichord when the solo part is also played on a modern instrument. Great care must be taken lest the piano overpower the recorder, and the sustaining pedal should be used very sparingly if at all.

Chamber Organ

A small chamber organ is an excellent alternative to the harpsichord for accompanying the descant recorder in early baroque sonatas, but does not combine well with the treble as its tone is too similar.

Plucked instruments

The five course baroque guitar and larger members of the lute family, such as the theorbo, provide excellent continuo accompaniment, having an expressive flexibility which the harpsichord lacks, and are particularly effective in French music. The modern Spanish or 'classical' guitar can also sound very good and, if less authentic, has the merits of versatility and availability.

The question of whether or not to double the bass line of the basso continuo needs careful consideration, especially where the solo instrument is as light and unassertive as the recorder. A bass viol or baroque cello combines well with a harpsichord and can balance with a single recorder, but regular rehearsal is necessary to achieve a satisfactory tonal blend and really precise ensemble between all three instruments. A modern cello is too heavy to balance with the recorder unless it is exceptionally delicately and sensitively played. If the piano has to be used for continuo accompaniment further strengthening of the bass line is quite unnecessary. The use of a cello or bass viol without a keyboard is another possibility which is both effective and historically authentic.

PLATE IV: Recorders, theorbo and baroque cello.

(Photo: Richmond & Twickenham Times Ltd.) *Reproduced by permission*

PLATE V: Recorder, bass viol and harpsichord

(Photo: Constantine) *Reproduced by permission*

The possibility of tuning a harpsichord or chamber organ in some form of unequal temperament also merits consideration. The advantage of meantone temperament was that it provided pure intonation in a restricted range of tonalities. The numerous variants of this method of tuning which were adopted in the seventeenth and early eighteenth centuries sought a compromise which enlarged the range of available tonalities while retaining pure or nearly pure major thirds in the less remote scales. Baroque recorders (see above) were built to accord with a keyboard instrument so tuned, and even a modern recorder can be made to do so by a skilled player. Most professional piano tuners are unfamiliar with any method of tuning other than equal temperament so a harpsichordist interested in early tunings and temperaments must learn to tune his own instrument.

Once the problems of instrumentation and tuning have been resolved, there remains the even more important question of the actual notes of the accompaniment. Although most modern editions of baroque music include a full realization of the figured bass it is preferable for the accompanist to devise his own part, just as the soloist should devise his own ornamentation, as this is what gives life and individuality to a performance. There is much to be said for improvizing, but it must be remembered that in the eighteenth century playing from a figured bass was the standard method of learning harmony. This is no longer so, and in the absence of a living tradition of figured bass playing it is often preferable to use a written accompaniment.

The mechanics of figured bass are fairly simple. A root position chord on the bass note is played unless figures indicate intervals other than the third and fifth; the figure 6 alone implies a sixth and a third; chromatic intervals are indicated by accidentals qualifying the figures. The performer has to ensure that any dissonance implied by the figures is correctly prepared and resolved and that consecutive fifths and octaves between the outer parts are avoided. However, merely fulfilling these requirements will not necessarily produce a good accompaniment. It is impossible to formulate an infallible set of rules for continuo accompaniment as so much depends on personal taste. Opinions differed in the baroque period as now, but as a rule of thumb guide and basis for further study and practical experiment the following points should be considered:

i) The function of continuo accompaniment is to enhance and clarify what is implicit in the composition. There is no point in turning a solo sonata into a trio sonata by the addition of ingenious counter-melodies. Generally the rhythm of the right-hand part should not be more complex than the bass line.

ii) The figures can sometimes safely be ignored. They were often the work of publishers rather than composers and if slavishly followed may produce bizarre effects.

iii) Ornaments in the solo part involving dissonance and resolution should not be doubled in the accompaniment.

iv) The accompaniment should not rise above the solo melody unless a point of imitation makes this necessary.

The Twentieth Century

I Repertoire

Of the large quantity of music written for the recorder in the present century a relatively small proportion is intended for concert performance at a professional level. Concerning the solo repertoire alone, it is convenient to distinguish between those works which require conventional playing techniques, without necessarily being traditional in idiom, and those which exploit the recorder's potential for new technical devices.

(a) Technically conventional works

In the early days of the recorder revival many composers, especially in England, wrote solo works, often at the invitation of the players and teachers most concerned with establishing the recorder as a concert instrument (see Edgar Hunt, *The Recorder and its Music*, pp. 140-141). Some of the music of that period adopted a consciously antique or folky style in deference to the recorder's supposed technical limitations, but many works have weathered well and are perhaps unjustly neglected. One reason for this neglect may be the difficulty of securing a good balance when the recorder is accompanied by the piano, but the two instruments are by no means incompatible and their joint repertoire is well worth exploring.

(b) *Avant garde* works

The term *avant garde* is adopted for convenience to describe those works which demand unconventional methods of performance (see Section 6). The very simplicity of the recorder's construction necessitates a highly sophisticated playing technique, and in this paradox lies the attraction of the instrument for experimental composers. In recent years a substantial quantity of stimulating recorder music has been written, much of which is dedicated to the Dutch virtuoso Frans Brüggen. There are some works with piano but composers tend to prefer to write for the recorder unaccompanied. There is a remarkable variety of scope and idiom in such works, and the term *avant garde* should not be assumed to imply a uniformity of style.

The serious student cannot afford to ignore recent developments in recorder music and should not be discouraged by the extreme difficulty of much of the *avant garde* repertoire. The music is exciting and rewarding to work on and the difficulties do lessen with experience and perseverance.

II Style

The music of the present day clearly presents the performer with fewer stylistic problems than that of the past. Where there is no necessity to recreate past traditions and conventions in the pursuit of an authentic style of performance, musicians can more safely trust their subjective reactions and allow their interpretation to be moulded by musical instinct. The situation is complicated slightly for recorder players by the recorder's decline into obsolescence in the second half of the eighteenth century and the consequent lack of an unbroken tradition of recorder playing. Because of the recorder's strong associations with the music of bygone eras, composers and performers alike may be tempted to approach the instrument as a historical curiosity.

In some respects the more conventional music is more difficult to perform convincingly than the *avant garde* repertoire, which creates its own atmosphere, is explicit in its technical demands and unambiguous in its relationship to the historic role of the recorder, at once antipathetical and complementary. The expressive demands of the conventional recorder and piano repertoire offer a challenge to the technical resources of both players. The recorder must achieve a subtlety of nuance, comparable to that of the piano by use of shading, alternative fingerings and imaginative use of vibrato and variety of articulation, while the piano must keep to a realistic dynamic level without sacrificing its natural expressive flexibility. The balance is a delicate one and can only be achieved by a sensitive and sympathetic partnership.

2 Early fingering systems

The following table is based on the fingering charts of three important writers on the recorder:

SYLVESTRO DI GANASSI *Opera intitulata Fontegara* (Venice, 1535)
JACQUES HOTTETERRE *Principes de la flûte traversière, ou flûte d'Allemagne; de la flûte à bec, ou flûte douce, et du haut-bois* (Paris, 1707)
THOMAS STANESBY JNR *A new system of the flute a'bec, or common English Flute* (London, ?1732)

Ganassi's and Stanesby's charts were for the recorder in C and have here been transposed into F for ease of comparison with Hotteterre. It is interesting that only Stanesby distinguishes between the fingerings for enharmonic notes. Hotteterre *does* make such distinctions in his fingering chart for the traverse flute, perhaps indicating that he was more familiar with that instrument than with the recorder, while Ganassi's alternative fingerings for some notes may suggest ways of tempering the intonation or of managing the idiosyncrasies of individual instruments or both.

Notice Hotteterre's use of finger 6 to support the instrument—the so-called 'buttress-finger' technique; notice also that Stanesby's fingerings for low A sharp and B flat seem to have been reversed. A sharp should be the flatter note.

Hotteterre's table of trill fingerings should also be closely studied (see the list of Suggestions for further study, Section 7). Trills between notes a semitone apart begin with the correct fingering for the upper note, but the fingering is then adjusted to enlarge the interval between the two notes.

	F	F♯	G♭	G	G♯	A♭	A	A♯	B♭	B	C♭
GANASSI	0 1 2 3 4 5 6 7	0 1 2 3 4 5 6 7̸		0 1 2 3 4 5 6 -	0 1 2 3 4 5 6̸ -		0 1 2 3 4 5 - -		0 1 2 3 4 - 6 -	0 1 2 3 - 5 6 7	
HOTTETERRE	0 1 2 3 4 5 6 7	0 1 2 3 4 5 6 7̸	0 1 2 3 4 5 6 7̸	0 1 2 3 4 5 6 -	0 1 2 3 4 5 6̸ -	0 1 2 3 4 5 6̸ -	0 1 2 3 4 5 - -	0 1 2 3 4 - 6 -	0 1 2 3 4 - 6 -	0 1 2 3 - 5 6 7	
STANESBY	0 1 2 3 4 5 6 7	0 1 2 3 4 5 6 7̸	0 1 2 3 4 5 6 7̸	0 1 2 3 4 5 6 -	0 1 2 3 4 5 6̸ 7	0 1 2 3 4 5 6̸ -	0 1 2 3 4 5 - -	0 1 2 3 4 - 6 7	0 1 2 3 4 5̸ 6 7	0 1 2 3 - 5 6 7	0 1 2 3 - 5 6 -

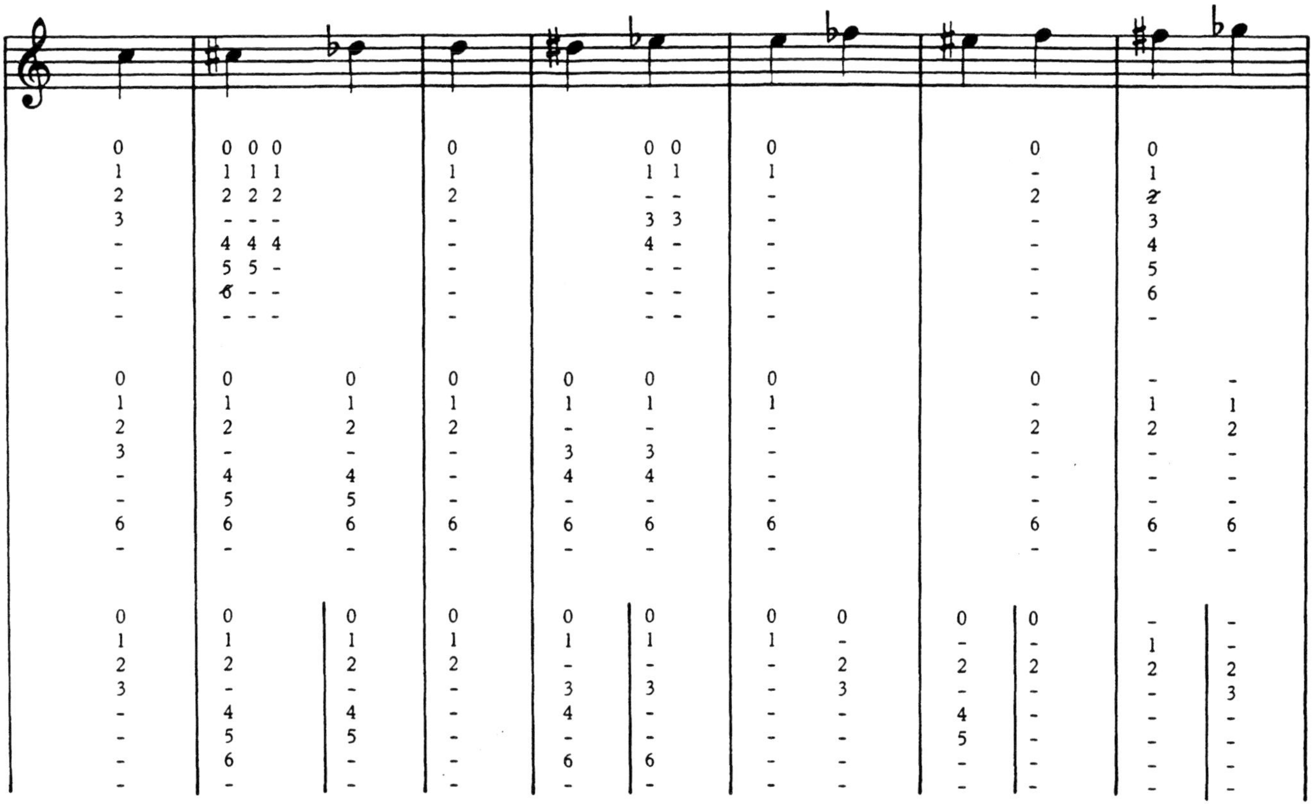

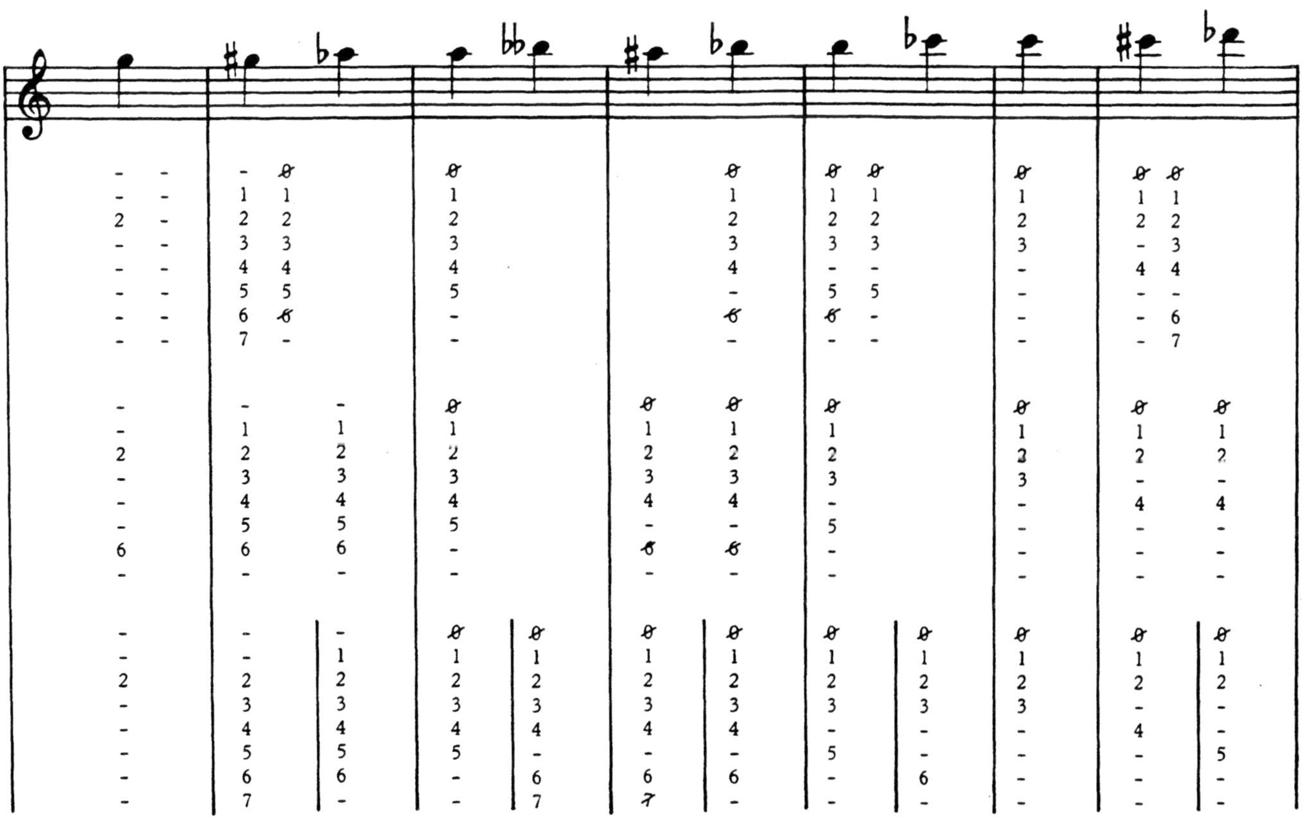

0	0	0	0	0	0	0	0	0	0
1	1	1	1	1	1	1	1	-	1
2	2	2	2	2	-	-	-	2	2̸
3	-	-	-	-	3	3	-	-	3
-	4	4	4	-	4	-	-	-	4
-	5	5	-	-	-	-	-	-	5
-	6̸	-	-	-	-	-	-	-	6
-	-	-	-	-	-	-	-	-	-

0	0	0	0	0	0	0	0	-	-
1	1	1	1	1	1	1	-	1	1
2	2	2	2	-	-	-	2	2	2
3	-	-	-	3	3	-	-	-	-
-	4	4	-	4	4	-	-	-	-
-	5	5	-	-	-	-	-	-	-
6	6	6	6	6	6	6	6	6	6
-	-	-	-	-	-	-	-	-	-

0	0	0	0	0	0	0	0	0	0	-	-
1	1	1	1	1	1	1	-	-	-	1	-
2	2	2	2	-	-	-	2	2	2	2	2
3	-	-	-	3	3	-	3	-	-	-	3
-	4	4	-	4	-	-	-	4	-	-	-
-	5	5	-	-	-	-	-	5	-	-	-
-	6	-	-	6	6	-	-	-	-	-	-
-	-	-	-	-	-	-	-	-	-	-	-

-	-	-	0̸	0̸	0̸	0̸	0̸	0̸	0̸	0̸
-	-	1	1	1	1	1	1	1	1	1
2	-	2	2	2	2	2	2	2	2	2
-	-	3	3	3	3	3	3	3	-	3
-	-	4	4	4	4	-	-	-	4	4
-	-	5	5	5	-	5	5	-	-	-
-	-	6	6̸	-	6̸	6̸	-	-	-	6
-	-	7	-	-	-	-	-	-	-	7

-	-	-	0̸	0̸	0̸	0̸	0̸	0̸	0̸
-	1	1	1	1	1	1	1	1	1
2	2	2	2	2	2	2	2	2	2
-	3	3	3	3	3	3	3	-	-
-	4	4	4	4	4	-	-	4	4
-	5	5	5	-	-	5	-	-	-
6	6	6	-	6̸	6̸	-	-	-	-
-	-	-	-	-	-	-	-	-	-

-	-	-	0̸	0̸	0̸	0̸	0̸	0̸	0̸	0̸	0̸
-	-	1	1	1	1	1	1	1	1	1	1
2	2	2	2	2	2	2	2	2	2	2	2
-	3	3	3	3	3	3	3	3	3	-	-
-	4	4	4	4	4	4	-	-	-	4	-
-	5	5	5	-	-	-	5	-	-	-	5
-	6	6	-	6	6	6	-	6	-	-	-
-	7	-	-	7	7̸	-	-	-	-	-	-

ø	ø	ø	ø	ø	ø	ø	ø	ø	ø	ø	ø	ø
1	1	1	1	1	1	1	1	1	1	-	-	-
2	2	-	-	-	-	~~2~~	-	-	-	2	2	2
-	-	3	3	-	-	3	3	3	3	3	3	3
-	4	-	-	-	-	4	4	4	4	~~4~~	4	-
-	~~5~~	5	5	5	-	5	5	-	5	5	-	5
-	-	6	6	6	6	6	6	6	6	6	-	-
-	-	7	~~7~~	-	-	7	~~7~~	-	-	7	-	-

ø	ø	ø	ø	ø	ø
1	1	1	1	1	1
2	2	2	2	-	-
-	-	-	-	-	3
-	-	-	4	4	4
-	5	5	5	5	-
-	6	6	-	-	6
-	7	7	-	-	7

ø	ø	ø	ø	ø	ø	ø	ø	ø
1	1	1	1	1	1	1	1	1
2	2	2	2	-	-	-	-	-
-	-	-	-	-	-	3	3	3
-	4	4	4	4	4	4	4	4
-	5	5	5	5	5	5	-	-
-	6	6	-	6	6	-	6	6
-	7	-	-	-	-	7	7	-

ø	ø	ø	ø	ø	ø	ø	ø	ø	ø	ø	ø	ø	ø
-	-	1	1	1	1	1	1	1	1	1	1	1	1
2	2	2	2	-	-	-	~~2~~	2	2	-	-	-	-
3	3	3	-	-	-	3	3	3	3	3	3	-	3
-	-	4	-	-	-	4	4	-	4	4	-	-	-
-	5	5	5	5	~~5~~	5	5	-	-	5	5	-	5
-	6	6	-	-	-	6	6	-	6	-	-	-	6
-	7	7	-	-	-	-	7	7	7	-	-	-	7

GANASSI

3 Articulation in renaissance and baroque music

The modern technique of single and double tonguing described in Part I can be supplemented by study of the variety of double tonguing syllables recommended by early writers on the recorder and other wind instruments. Early techniques of articulation are particularly useful when playing old instruments (or copies) since they provide a subtlety of expression which disappeared with the mechanization of the modern woodwind and the increased dynamic range of the instruments. Modern double tonguing (D-G or T-K) is a technical device which ideally should be indistinguishable from fast single tonguing; renaissance and baroque musicians adopted a fundamentally different attitude by exploiting the inequalities inherent in any double tonguing system. This is particularly evident in relation to French baroque music, but is implied by most writers on the subject. A thorough exploration of the possibilities of early articulation systems requires a detailed study of the original writers (see Section 7), but such study should be practical rather than theoretical. The following explanations and examples are intended as an introduction to the subject. The examples should be practised using the articulation suggested, though it may prove more profitable to work on just one system at a time using material from the standard repertoire.

I Le re Le re

This is the standard articulation for the 'passagi', the improvised or written decorations in renaissance music. It is a very smooth articulation but distinct from a true legato. Though difficult to master, it produces a fine effect which cannot be achieved with any other method of tonguing.

EXERCISES

KING HENRY VIII *If Love Now Reigned* (top line from a three-part piece)

CIPRIANO DE RORE *Beato me dire* (part of the top line of a four-part madrigal with decorations by Girolamo Dalla Casa)
(Recorder in C)

II Did'll Did'll

This form of double tonguing is recommended by Quantz for the traverse flute principally in passage work which moves by step.

J. J. QUANTZ *Versuch einer Anweisung die Flöte traversiere zu spielen*, Chapter VI, Section III/7

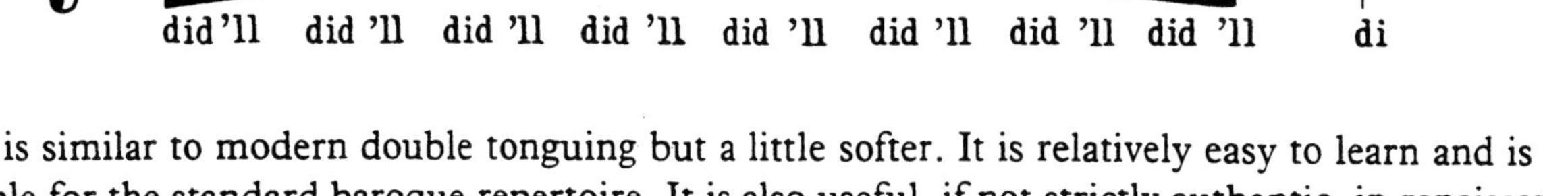

Its effect is similar to modern double tonguing but a little softer. It is relatively easy to learn and is indispensable for the standard baroque repertoire. It is also useful, if not strictly authentic, in renaissance music.

EXERCISES

JACOB VAN EYCK *Pavana lacryme* from 'Der Fluyten Lust-hof', 1646, (Final Variation)

(Recorder in C)

WILLIAM CORBET Prelude from 'Select Preludes and Vollentaries for the Flute . . .', 1708. (The marking in bar 3 is original)

ARCANGELO CORELLI *La Follia* (Version for Recorder and Continuo, 1702, Recorder part only)

Bars 97-112

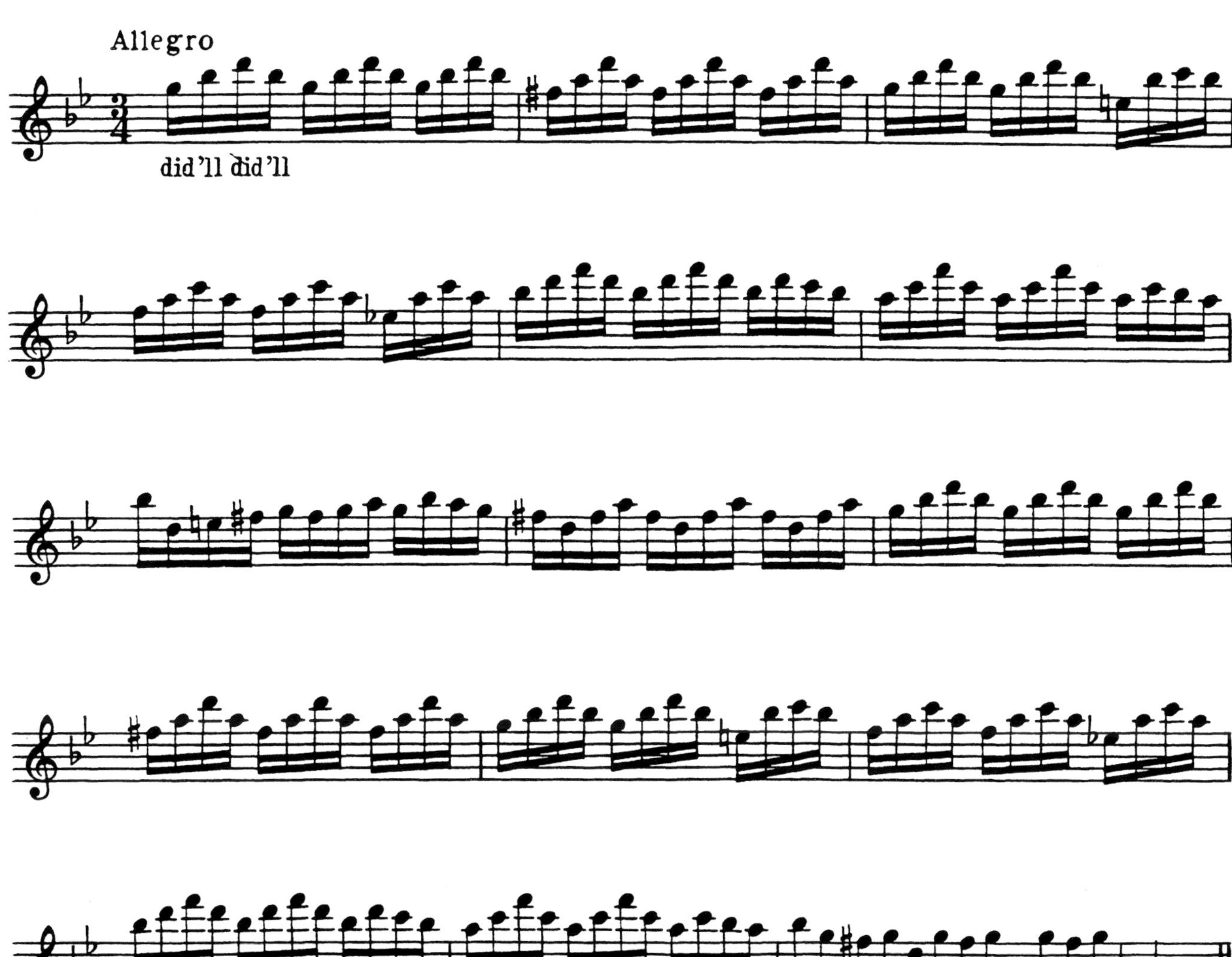

Bars 314-329

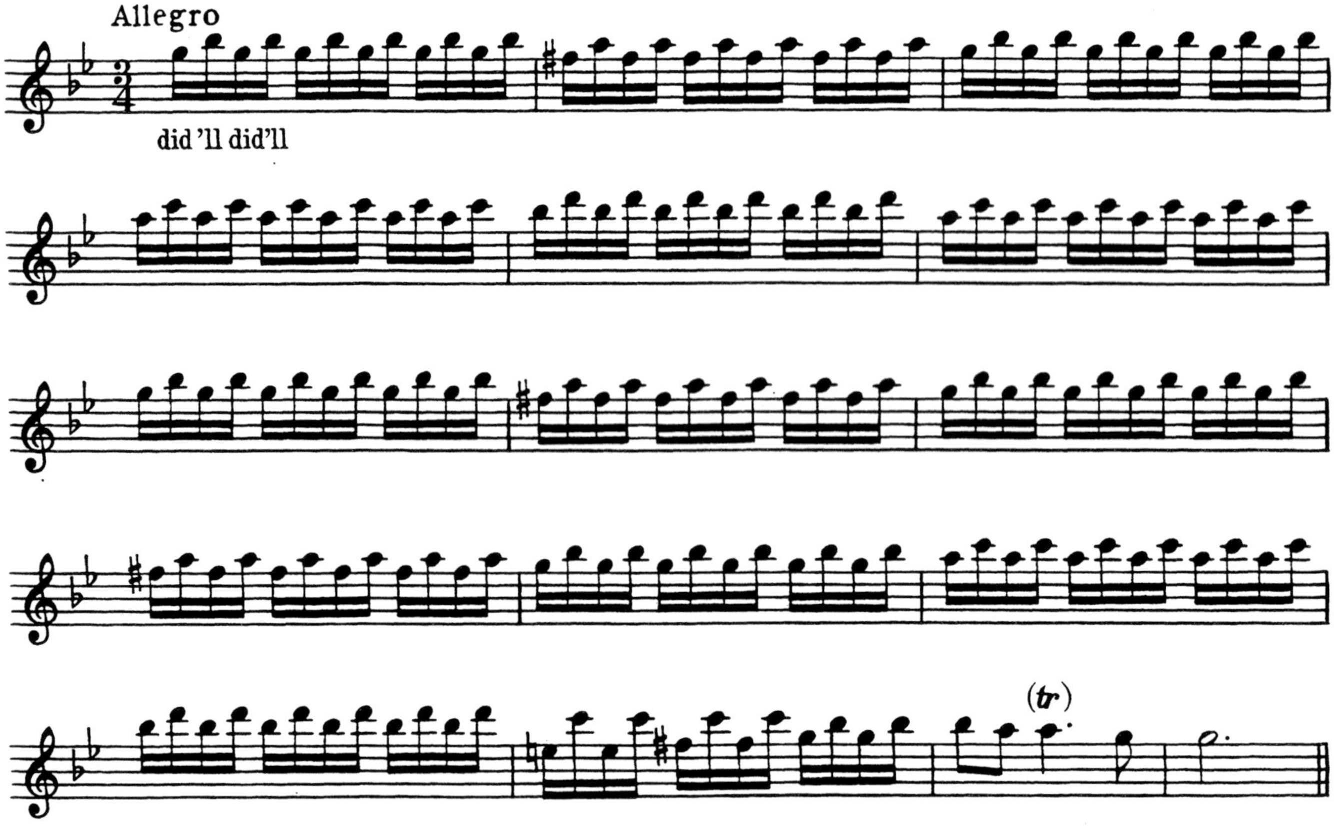

Allegro

did 'll did'll

(tr)

III Tu tu ru tu

This tonguing is specified by Hotteterre (*Principes de la flûte traversière* . . . 1707) in various contexts, but particularly for those notes which according to French tradition were played unequally although notated in equal note values.

JACQUES HOTTETERRE *Principes de la flûte traversière*, Chapter 8

The syllable 'ru' is pronounced as in modern English, not in the throat as in modern French (see David Lasocki's introduction to his translation of the *Principes* . . . , page 19). Quantz gives a very similar articulation for dotted notes.

J. J. QUANTZ *Versuch einer Anweisung die Flöte traversiere zu spielen,* Chapter VI, Section II/5

(Fig. 10)

Notes Inégales were a distinctive feature of French baroque instrumental style. A subtle lilt was achieved by placing a quantitative stress on certain notes in a way which, like the rhythmic nuances of jazz musicians, is incapable of notation. The conventions governing inequality are complicated and musicians of the period did not always agree. Nevertheless the basic principles may be summarized as follows:

i) The shortest note values to appear in significant numbers in a movement are usually taken unequally, particularly when they move by step.
ii) Notes slurred in pairs, repeated notes and large intervals are normally taken equally, but may be played unequally to conform to a prevailing pattern on inequality.
iii) Qualifying words indicating inequality (*inégale, pointé, piqué, louré*) or equality (*égale, détaché, martelé*) override the above.
iv) The degree of inequality may vary within a single movement.

Both Hotteterre and Quantz were concerned primarily with the traverse flute, and while their advice on articulation is also relevant to the recorder, 'tu tu ru tu' (or 'ti ti ri ti') can sound indistinct on the recorder, or give the impression of slurs from the weak to the strong note.

This can easily be overcome by slightly hardening the 'ru' syllable or modifying the articulation to 'tu tu *du* tu'.

EXERCISE

JACQUES HOTTETERRE Allemande from 'Première Suitte de Pièces à deux Dessus, sans Basse Contenue', 1712

Play the slurred pairs equally. The sign + indicates trill (see Section 4); other ornaments have been omitted.

IV Slurs

The slurring together of groups of rapid notes was certainly done in the sixteenth century, but contemporary writers who referred to the practice did so only to condemn it. The deliberate use of the slur was part of the expressive vocabulary of baroque music and could be introduced at the discretion of the performer when not specified by the composer, but indiscriminate use of slurs to ease the effort of articulation or even to produce variety for its own sake is contrary to baroque practice. The slur is perhaps best thought of as an ornament whose function, like that of other baroque ornaments, is to enhance and clarify the content and aesthetic character of the music. Study of composers' original slurs is of course helpful in establishing familiarity with good slurring practice, but it is worth remembering that often composers may have taken more trouble to indicate exceptional use of slurs, entrusting more conventional usage to the taste of the player.

EXERCISES

In the following examples original slurs are shown in the normal way while suggested slurs are indicated with a broken line.

J. S. BACH *Andante* from Brandenburg Concerto No.4 in G (BWV 1049, Fiauto d'Echo 1 and 2)

This extract illustrates three important uses of the slur:

i) To emphasize the grouping of notes in pairs.
ii) To enclose a florid, cadenza-like ornamental figure (bars 29 and 31).
iii) To join a dissonant note to its ensuing resolution (bars 14 and 15 and 40-2).

Bars 1-44

f
p
f
tr
tr
p
f
p
f
tr
tr
tr

G. P. TELEMANN Sonata in C for recorder and continuo (Essercizii Musici, 1740) 1st movement (recorder part only)

The slurs in the *adagio* sections of this movement are again to emphasize the expressive grouping of notes in pairs; in the *allegros* the slurs are suggested principally to clarify the melodic structure (beginning at the end of bar 12).

JACQUES HOTTETERRE Suite in D minor from Deuxième livre de Pièces pour la Flûte et autres instruments, 1715

In French baroque music the slur has extra significance as it affects the conventions of inequality. As already explained, notes slurred in pairs are normally taken equally; where they descend by step (e.g. bar 3) the inequality may even be reversed to produce a snapped rhythm. The French word *coulé* is used with its literal meaning of 'slur' and also to describe this kind of reversed inequality.

Rondeau – *gay* (recorder part only)

JACQUES HOTTETERRE Musette from Deuxième Suitte de Pièces à deux Dessus, sans Basse Contenue, 1717

This piece illustrates the exceptional combination of inequality with slurs. The grouping of the notes in fours rather than twos is even more likely to discourage inequality, hence the composer's explicit instruction not to follow the normal convention.

tr
tr
tr
tr
D.𝄋 al Fin
tr

4 Improvization and ornamentation in renaissance and baroque music

In a sense every musical performance includes an element of improvization as no two performances are ever identical in every nuance, but at certain stages in the historical development of musical performance stylistic convention has demanded a technique of improvization extending beyond the limits of expressive detail to include the content of the music itself. Renaissance musicians cultivated the art of 'dividing' the notes of a melody into shorter notes to form variations or 'divisions'. This tradition of decorative improvization survived throughout the seventeenth century and became particularly associated with the bass viol. In the baroque period keyboard players were accustomed to improvizing accompaniments from a figured bass and for singers and instrumentalists the addition of stylized ornamentation to a melodic line was part of the expressive rhetoric of solo performance.

Sadly, improvization is no longer generally regarded as a basic musical skill except in certain specialized fields, and while there is no doubt that genuine improvization in any idiom generates a unique feeling of exhilaration, many present-day musicians, obliged to perform in a variety of idioms, feel uneasy about improvizing on the concert platform. A further difficulty arises in recording, as it is virtually impossible to maintain a consistent style of improvization throughout a series of re-takes. What matters most is that any ornamentation, whether improvized, semi-improvized or preconceived in some detail, should *sound* spontaneous and fresh.

I Renaissance divisions

The most frequent use of division in renaissance music is to decorate the leading note in cadences. The degree of complexity will depend on the context, but the following formulae can be memorized, practised in various keys and applied extempore to appropriate cadences.

Dividing a melody requires the breaking down of notes into smaller values to produce a more elaborate line, perhaps with new rhythmic interest, while maintaining the strict regard for dissonance and consonance characteristic of sixteenth century counterpoint. In ensemble music it is necessary to pre-arrange which part will be decorated and the player responsible must be aware of the other part or parts, either by playing from a score or through careful preparation.

ORLANDO DI LASSO *Bicinium* (1610)

The suggested ornamentation illustrates some of the principles discussed above. The original parts are in normal size notes with the ornamentation superimposed in small notes so that alternative and additional divisions can be devised. In this version ornamentation has been added to both parts, but not of course at the same time. Another method would be to leave one part plain and to ornament the other throughout.

TIELMAN SUSATO Pavan (after Josquin des Pres, *Danserye*, 1551)

This dance is printed in full in playing score to facilitate extempore ornamentation of any of the four parts. Any notes forming a dissonance with the bass (i.e. seconds, fourths, sevenths and their compounds) should normally be either passing notes or suspensions. Divisions of the bass line itself should not produce the effect of 'second inversion' chords. Consecutive fifths and octaves must also be avoided.

*The high E in bar 14 is outside the range of some 'renaissance' treble recorders in F but is possible on the more authentic G instrument.

Suggested openings for improvized or written divisions of the top part:

II Baroque ornamentation

By the second half of the seventeenth century stylized conventions of extempore ornamentation had developed. Performers were judged not only on execution, tone and phrasing but also on their ability to embellish a melodic line with appropriate graces. Baroque ornamentation is a complex subject requiring detailed study of both original sources and later scholarly comment, but the sheer volume of documentation should not inhibit attempts by the beginner to add simple ornamentation to a sonata slow movement. It is important, however, to distinguish from the outset between the French and Italian styles which represent opposite poles in baroque performance practice; musicians of the time were keenly aware of the difference, but subsequent musical developments have inevitably blunted this awareness for the modern musician. The rhythmic conventions of French baroque music and their relationship to techniques of articulation have been referred to in Section 3. The following remarks on ornamentation are intended as a practical guide to basic aspects of the subject and for that reason little reference has been made to supporting documentary evidence. Clearly this approach may lead to oversimplification: there are exceptions to every rule and musical commonsense should always prevail over dogmatic adherence to academic correctness.

(a) French baroque ornamentation

French composers tended to notate their ornamentation, leaving little scope for the invention of the performer. The harpsichord suites of François Couperin provide the most comprehensive guide to French ornamentation and should be closely studied. The signs used for ornaments varied between different composers, but there was a remarkable consistency in the use of particular ornaments in characteristic contexts. Where composers left melodic lines undecorated the performer should aim to supply appropriate graces. The following illustrations of the principal ornaments of French baroque music are taken from Hotteterre's two collections of *Pièces pour la Flûte Traversière* (1715) and have been transposed to suit the recorder; both melody and bass are given so that the harmonic effect of the ornaments may be appreciated; the ornaments are shown in small notes, except for the trill which has its familiar modern abbreviation ***tr***, in preference to the composer's original signs which are likely to be unfamiliar to many beginners. For the sake of clarity, in each example ornaments other than the one under consideration have been omitted.

The *tremblement* (trill)

The trill is used almost invariably on the supertonic or leading note in perfect cadences both within and at the end of a movement. The cadential trill begins with the upper note which is sounded on the beat to form a dissonance with the bass and ends with an anticipation of the tonic which is usually indicated in the notation:

Suite No.4, Book 2
Courante – *gay*

played

N.B. The initial upper note is not shown in the notation. Its presence is implied by the abbreviation ***tr*** or any of the many other trill signs used in baroque music of all nationalities. If a trill is added to a note which is itself already dissonant with the bass, the initial upper note should still be played but made very short and perhaps even before the beat:

Suite No. 2, Book 1
Sarabande: *La Guimon*

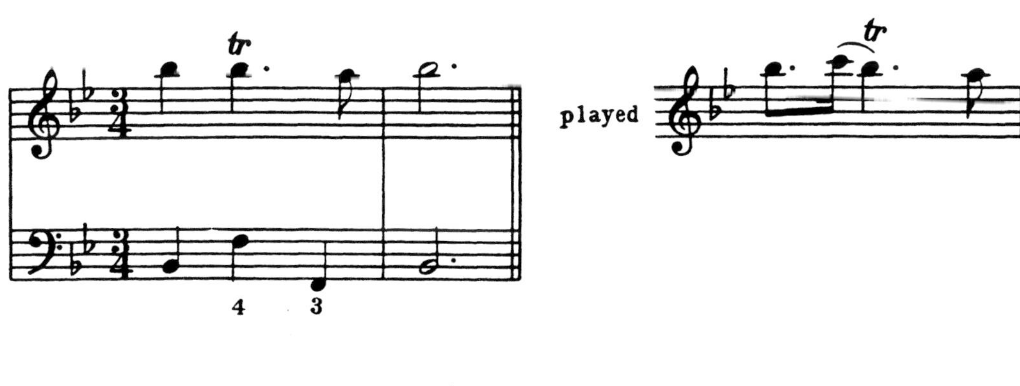

The *battement* or *pincé* (mordent)

The mordent is used to give emphasis to a note approached by leap, usually from below:

Suite No. 4, Book 1
Air: *Le Fleuri*

The *port de voix* (lower appoggiatura) 

The lower appoggiatura occurs on notes approached from below by step. It is played on the beat, strongly accented and may be followed by a mordent:

Suite No. 2, Book 2
Allemande – *tendrement*

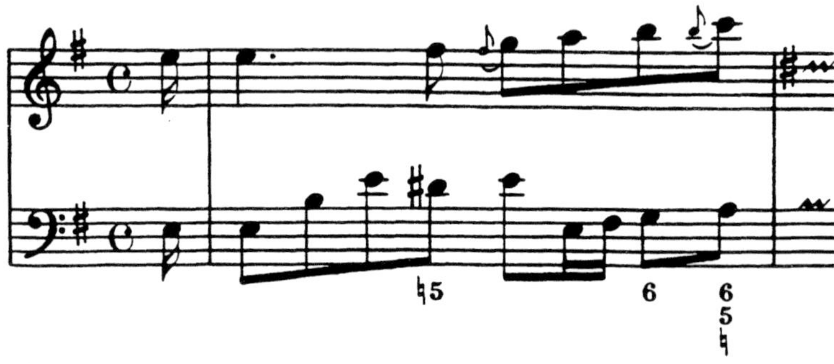

The *coulement* (passing appoggiatura) 

This is a grace note between two main notes which descend a third. It is played *before* the beat but slurred on to the second note. Its most characteristic context is at the end of a phrase following a short trill or other ornament on the first main note:

Suite No. 1, Book 1
Gavotte: *La Meudon*

The *accent* (springer)

The *accent* is an upper auxiliary note between two main notes of the same pitch, the first usually being dotted. It is slurred from the first note. The *accent* is very expressive and characteristic but should be used sparingly as its effect can pall.

Suite No. 1, Book 1
Prélude – *lentement*

The *flattement* (fingered vibrato)
The *flattement* was seldom notated but was a notable feature of French baroque woodwind technique. It was particularly associated with the traverse flute but sounds effective on the recorder also. The effect is produced by fingering the edge or shading open holes to make a fingered vibrato on the flat side of the main note which should, of course, begin and end in tune. The *flattement* can be applied to any note of sufficient length and should always be used in preference to breath vibrato in French music.

These ornaments by no means exhaust the possibilities but they are the ones most frequently used and most characteristic of the French style, and will form the basis of a good working vocabulary which can be extended as experience and confidence increase. The use of facsimiles and good modern editions will help to achieve familiarity with the original notation used by various composers.

EXERCISES

These dance movements by Hotteterre are given with the original ornamentation. They should be practised until the style feels comfortable, then used as models for the similar movements by Dieupart, originally unornamented.

HOTTETERRE Menuet: *Le Comte de Brione* from Suite No. 1, Book 1

DIEUPART Menuet from Suite in C, originally A

HOTTETERRE Gavotte – *tendrement* from Suite No. 2, Book 2

(b) Italian Baroque Ornamentation

Italian baroque music demands a much freer, more improvizatory approach to ornamentation than French. The cadential trill occurs in Italian music as in French, and many of the individual ornaments used by French composers can be used in appropriate contexts in Italian music, but the Italian style also requires, in slow movements at least, an element of free melodic invention. Some slow movements, indeed, were written in such a skeletal form that without fairly substantial embellishment they are virtually meaningless.

As with renaissance music, in public performance an appropriate compromise between true improvization and precomposition must be found, according to the skill, temperament and inclination of the performer. In private practice, every recorder player should strive to develop the ability to improvize good ornamentation fluently and confidently. This requires some knowledge of harmony and an understanding of figured bass and, most important of all, the ability to play accurately by ear, an aspect of musicianship which is usually overlooked in conventional musical training.

The study of contemporary evidence in the form of treatises and written-out examples of ornamentation is also essential, but must not be allowed to inhibit a creative approach to the music. The stimulus should come from within the music itself, and the ornamentation should enhance the expressive content. To reproduce in performance even a well authenticated 'original' ornamented version of a sonata movement is only of historic interest and contrary to the spirit of Italian baroque music.

The following movement from a Handel sonata will be familiar to all recorder players. It provides an illustration of how ornamentation can be made to grow from the musical content, the details being decided by the performer in practice or performance.

G. F. HANDEL *Larghetto* from Sonata in F, Opus 1, No. 11

(a) The purpose of long notes of this kind is usually to free the ear to concentrate on the bass, so any ornamentation added must not be distracting so as to distort the contrapuntal balance. Discreet vibrato may be sufficient to keep the recorder line alive, especially if it is avoided elsewhere in the movement.

(b) The music is moving towards a small climax in bar 7. By breaking the crotchet movement the feeling of momentum can be increased.

The possibilities are, of course, infinite. The precise details and degree of complexity should ideally reflect the player's response to a specific performing context—allowing, for example, for the acoustics, the instruments being used, the character of the audience, the position in the programme and many less tangible factors.

(c) The importance of this note in the phrase can be enhanced by some kind of dissonant ornament: a trill or plain appoggiatura.

(d) This is a repetition of the opening material and any ornamentation should aim to reinforce this in the listener's ear by underlining the character of the melody. The use of turns and turned trills and anticipation can emphasize the gradual stepwise ascent of the melody and this can be nicely balanced by the use of grace notes (*coulements*) or appoggiature to decorate the descending thirds.

(e) Conventional cadential trills are required. The initial appoggiatura should be long and firmly played on the beat.

(f) A melodic sequence usually requires ornamentation whose effect is cumulative. It need not be elaborate, and must not obscure the original line.

(g) The conventional ending on the dominant chord is an opportunity for an improvized cadenza to lead into the following movement. The bass is static in the penultimate bar to allow freedom to the soloist. Here, above all, an element of genuine improvization is desirable as it heightens the rapport between the soloist and accompanist. A concluding trill signals the end of the cadenza.

Conclusion

There is an abundance of easily available study material in the form of facsimile and modern editions of early treatises as well as modern works of scholarship. The purpose of the present work, however, is to encourage an inventive and improvizatory approach to renaissance and baroque ornamentation and for that reason most of the examples of ornamentation have been specially written rather than culled from 'authentic' sources.

5 The French violin clef

The ability to read the French violin clef is very useful not only because it was the normal clef for the recorder in the eighteenth century and survives in certain collected editions but also because its substitution for the more familiar treble clef facilitates the upward transposition of a minor third necessary in playing music originally composed for the traverse flute (see Section 1).

EXERCISES

These exercises are taken from familiar works in the baroque repertoire, but are given with their original clefs and in their original keys.

J. S. BACH Concerto from Cantata No. 152 (recorder part only)

2
tr
4

G. P. TELEMANN Minuet from Suite in A minor (recorder part only)

Play the following exercises a minor third higher by substituting the French violin clef for the treble clef and adjusting accidentals where necessary.

J. S. BACH Allemande from Partita in A minor for solo flute (BWV 1013)

G. P. TELEMANN *Allegro* from Fantasia in G for solo flute

6 *Avant garde* techniques

Some recent recorder music requires a variety of unconventional technical devices. Generally speaking these techniques are still sufficiently new and unfamiliar to require composers' explanations in scores where they are employed, but certain of them recur sufficiently frequently to be identified and studied in isolation; moreover, some degree of uniformity in notation is gradually being established.

EXERCISES

The following exercises attempt to provide an introduction to the *avant garde* style by focusing on specific aspects of technique.

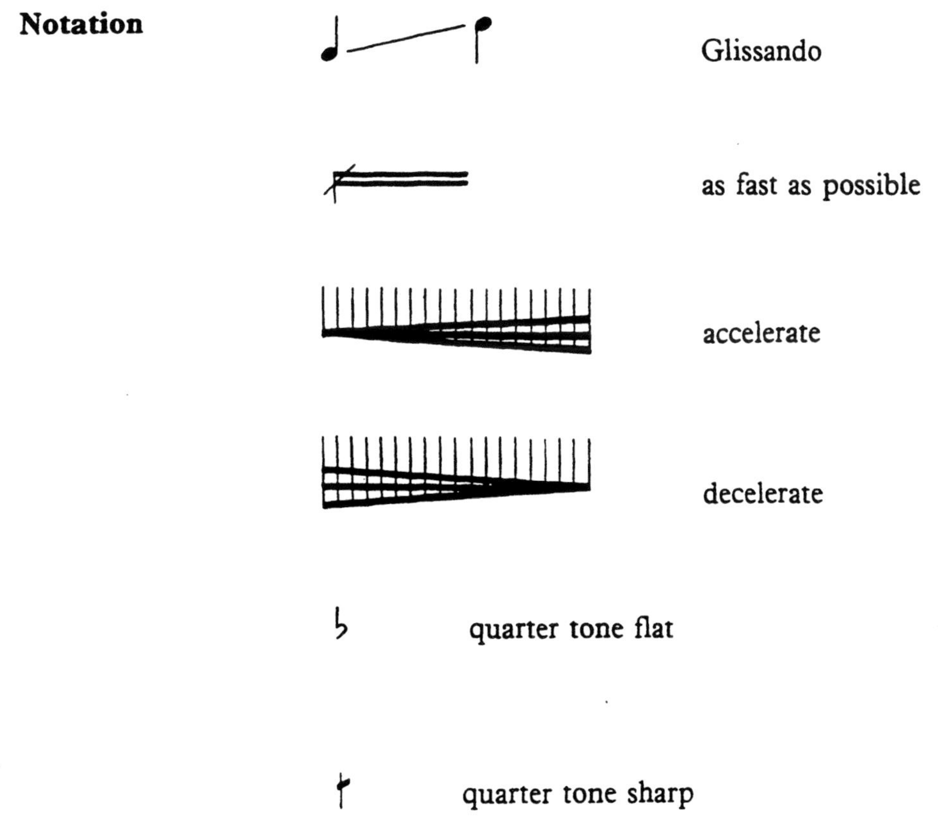

In unbarred pieces accidentals apply to single or repeated notes only.

(a) Rapid atonal groups

(b) Combined vocal and instrumental tone. The voice part should be pitched as accurately as possible either as written or an octave lower.

(c) Glissandi

(1) 0 - - - - - - - (2) 0 1 2 3 - - - - (3) 0 1 2 - - - - -

(d) Quarter tones

Table of suggested fingerings

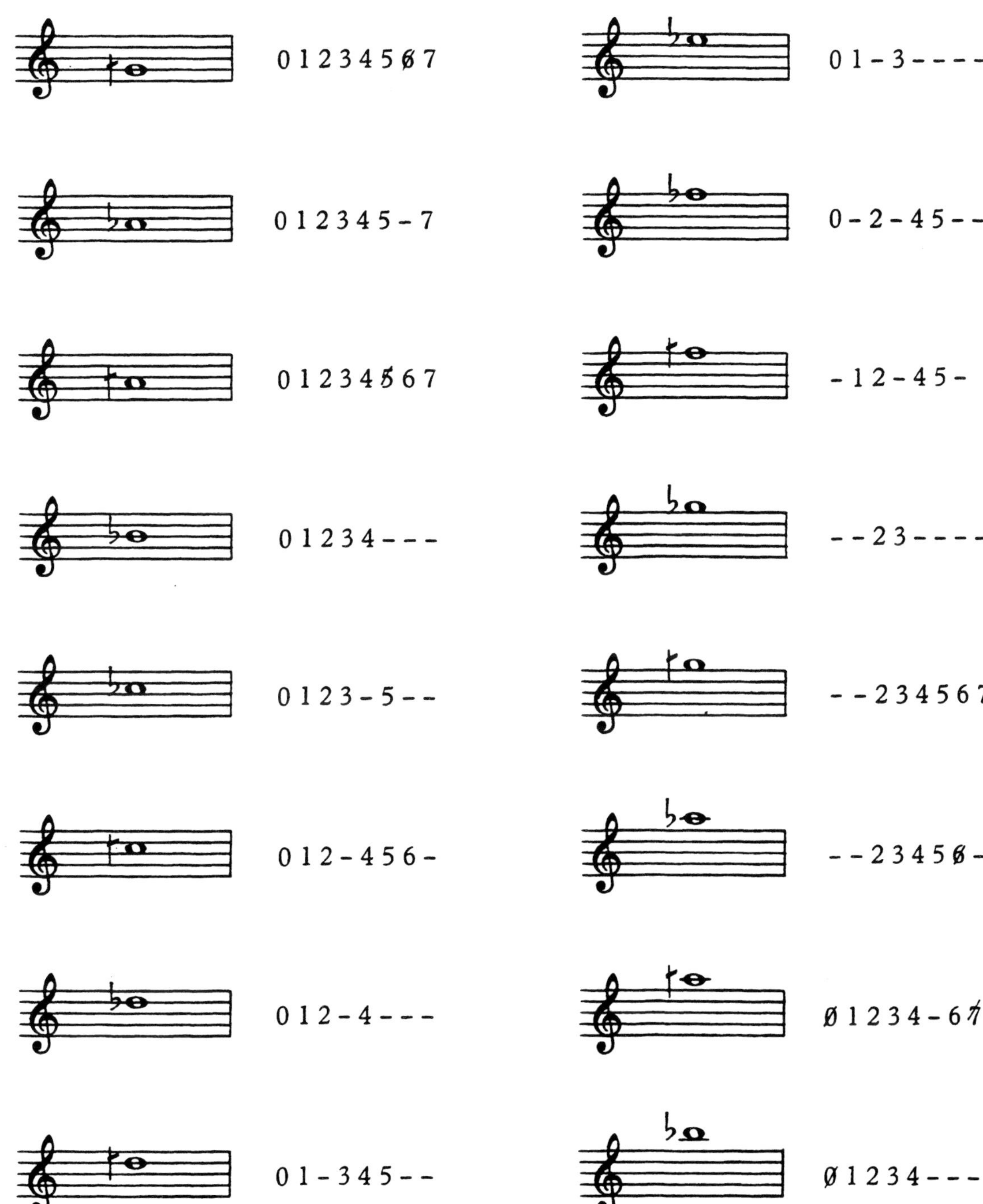

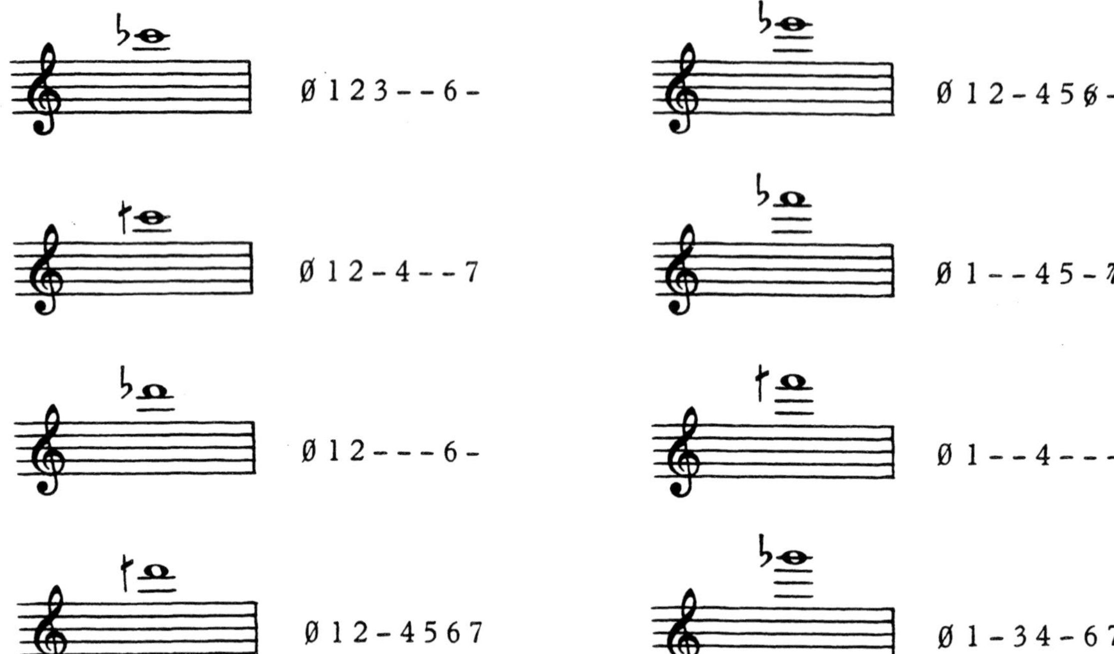
Ø 1 2 3 - - 6 -
Ø 1 2 - 4 - - 7
Ø 1 2 - - - 6 -
Ø 1 2 - 4 5 6 7
Ø 1 2 - 4 5 6̸ -
Ø 1 - - 4 5 - 7̸
Ø 1 - - 4 - - -
Ø 1 - 3 4 - 6 7

♩ = 60-66

(e) Chords

By overblowing it is possible to produce the effect of a 'chord' through the combined sound of a fundamental and a harmonic. For both notes to be audible the breath pressure must be just right and held very steady. The correct force of articulation must be found by trial and error; it frequently has to be stronger than is necessary for single notes.

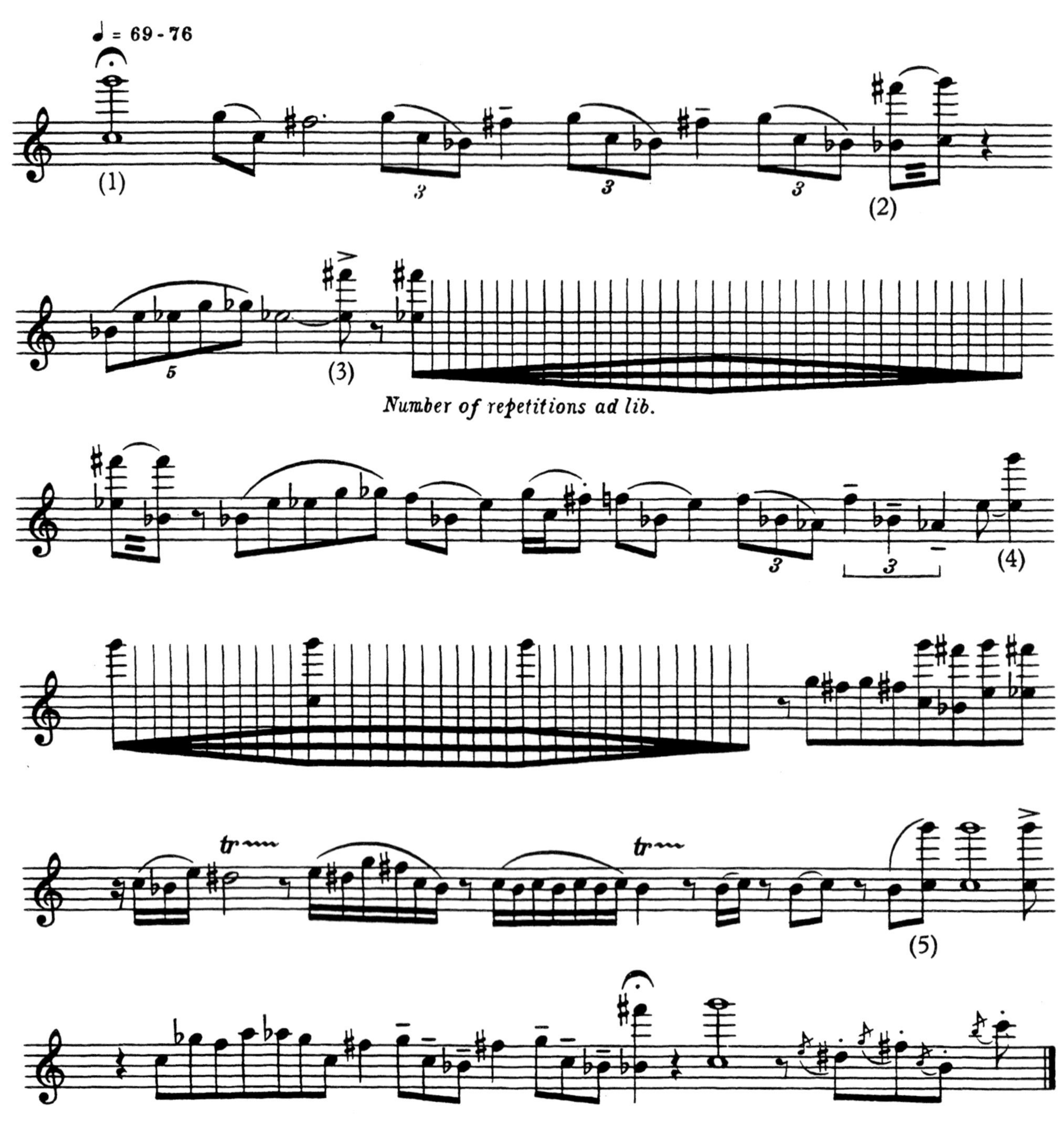

(1) 0 1 2 3 - - 6 7 (2) 0 1 2 3 4 - 6 7 (3) 0 1 - 3 4 - 6 7 (4) 0 1 - 3 - - 6 7 (5) 0 1 2 3 - 5 6 -

7 Suggestions for further study

The following list is highly selective. Rather than attempt to provide a comprehensive bibliography I have chosen a small number of essential works which may be regarded as required reading for the serious recorder student.

Technique

ROWLAND-JONES, A.	*Recorder Technique* (Oxford University Press)
VETTER, MICHAEL	*Il Flauto Dolce ed Acerbo* (Moeck)

Interpretation — modern works

BROWN, H. MAYER	*Embellishing 16th century music* (OUP)
DART, R. THURSTON	*The Interpretation of Music* (Hutchinson)
DOLMETSCH, ARNOLD	*The Interpretation of the Music of the XVIIth and XVIIIth Centuries revealed by Contemporary Evidence* (Novello)
DONINGTON, ROBERT	*The Interpretation of Early Music* (Faber)
EMERY, WALTER	*Bach's Ornaments* (Novello)
WESTRUP, JACK	*Musical Interpretation* (BBC)

Interpretation — early sources

GANASSI, SYLVESTRO DI (ed. H. Peter, tr. D. Swainson)	*Opera intitulata Fontegara* (Venice, 1535) (Robert Lienau)
HOTTETERRE, JACQUES (ed. and tr. D. Lasocki)	*Principes de la flûte traversière, ou flûte d'Allemagne; de la flûte à bec, ou flûte douce, et du haut-bois* (Paris, 1707) (Barrie and Rockliff)
QUANTZ, JOHANN JOACHIM (cd. and tr. E. R. Reilly)	*Versuch einer Anweisung die Flöte traversiere zu spielen* (Berlin, 1752) (Faber)

General

BAINES, ANTHONY	*Woodwind Instruments and their History* (Faber)
HUNT, EDGAR	*The Recorder and its Music* (Eulenberg)
MUNROW, DAVID	*Instruments of the Middle Ages and Renaissance* (OUP)
THOMSON, JOHN M.	*Your Book of the Recorder* (Faber)
WELCH, CHRISTOPHER (ed. E. Hunt)	*Lectures on the Recorder* (OUP)

Printed and bound in the United Kingdom

8/02 (45062)

Music for Recorder

Solo

Patrick Enfield

Descant's Delight

3 pieces for descant recorder and piano.

Gordon Saunders

Classical Solos

41 pieces for alto or treble recorder.

Eight Traditional Japanese Pieces

Selected and transcribed for tenor or descant recorder or flute.

Duet

Gordon Saunders

Classical Duets

24 graded pieces transcribed for alto (treble) and tenor recorder.

Ensemble

A W Benoy

Fifteen European Carols

Arranged in three parts:— descant 1, descant 2 or treble 1, treble 2 or tenor.

Ten European Folk Songs

Arranged in three parts:— descant 1, descant 2 or treble 1, treble 2 or tenor.

Elgar

Chanson de Matin

Arranged for descant, treble 1, treble 2, tenor & bass, by Dom Gregory Murray.

Fauré

Pavane

Arranged for descant, treble 1, treble 2, tenor 1, tenor 2, bass & optional great bass by Brian Davey.

609(83)